Develop your English

Reading

nec
NATIONAL
EXTENSION
COLLEGE

Reading

© 2002 National Extension College Trust Ltd. All rights reserved.

ISBN 1 84308 103 2

Author:	Bob Holt, Basic Skills Development Officer, Cambridge and Peterborough Learning Partnership
Consultants:	Morag Carmichael, Key and Basic Skills Consultant
	Sheila White, Open Learning Consultant
Project Manager:	Steve Attmore
Proof-reader:	Rebecca Norman
Cover design by:	CBA Design and Marketing
Photography by:	Mel Curtis/Getty Images and Jim Arbogast/Getty Images
Page design by:	John Matthews
Page layout by:	Deborah Matthews
Printed by:	Pear Tree Press Limited, Stevenage

Every effort has been made to contact the copyright holders of material reproduced here. The author and publisher wish to thank the following organisations for permission to reproduce copyright material: Guardian Newspapers for extract from July 1999.

The National Extension College is an educational trust and a registered charity with a distinguished body of Trustees. It is an independent, self-financing organisation. Since it was established in 1963 NEC has pioneered the development of flexible learning for adults. NEC is actively developing innovative materials and systems for open and distance learning opportunities on over 150 courses, from basic skills to degree and professional training.

For further details of NEC resources contact:

National Extension College Trust Ltd
The Michael Young Centre
Purbeck Road
Cambridge CB2 2HN
Tel 01223 400300 Fax 01223 400321
e-mail: resources@nec.ac.uk   website: http//www.nec.ac.uk

Contents

Introduction

Welcome to the workbook on reading. This workbook will help you to develop your ability to read. It should help you to:

- read and understand different types of writing
- read and obtain information from different types of writing.

The other 'Develop your English' workbooks available are:

- Writing
- Speaking and Listening (with accompanying CD).

Why reading matters to you

Reading is important in all areas of life. We are now having to take in a lot more information than 50 years ago and so it is becoming more, not less, important that we read well. In education, reading well is a skill needed for all subjects. At work, we have to read a wide range of material for a wide range of reasons.

Reading is a skill we all need in order to cope with everyday life, but at this level we must also be able to *read well*. This means being able to:

- read quickly
- say why what we are reading has been written
- recognise other people's opinions in what we read
- take information we need from what we read
- make judgements about what we read.

Remember, as you work through this module, that reading well will come with practice. It may feel like a slow process when you are first trying out your new reading skills, but you will definitely improve if you practise.

How to use the workbook

You have probably chosen this workbook because you, or a tutor, have identified the need for you to develop your reading skills.

This workbook is divided into 6 sections:

1 ways to read

2 reading different types of text

3 identifying the main points of a text

4 reading and understanding arguments

5 using a library

6 reading technical documents.

You can work through the sections in any order, but it is a good idea to start with Section 1 on ways to read.

Each section is divided into a number of short topics with activities designed to engage your imagination and promote fast, effective learning. Suggestions for the activities are provided, where appropriate. These are intended to help you to check that:

(a) you understand the concept involved

(b) show you can put the concept into practice.

These suggestions usually follow the activity. It is important that you check your answers with the suggestions provided, before continuing. It is also important that you attempt the questions on your own. Looking at the 'suggestions' before you try to solve the problem will NOT help your learning.

Key terms are printed in **bold**. Definitions of these terms appear in the Glossary section at the end of the workbook.

Hints/Notes
Handy hints and useful notes are provided as aids to memory.

Reflective learning log

In each topic there is at least one 'Reflective learning log' section. This is for you to create. You can make notes in your log of what you have learned in that particular topic. You can write down anything that you have found useful. This may be a handy hint, a formula or just a way of remembering how to do something. Use your 'learning log' to help with revision.

Resources

For your work on this book you will need the following:

	Section 1	Section 2	Section 3	Section 4	Section 5	Section 6
Highlighter pen(s)	✔	✔	✔	✔		✔
A modern dictionary of a reasonable size (e.g. *Concise Oxford Dictionary*)	✔	✔	✔	✔	✔	
Daily newspapers		✔*	✔	✔		
Access to a library					✔	
Watch or timer	✔		✔			

* You will need two daily newspapers – one popular newspaper (known as a **tabloid**), one more serious (known as a **broadsheet**).

The national standards for adult literacy

A national strategy to tackle the literacy needs of adults was launched by the government in Autumn 2000. The strategy includes:

● national standards for adult literacy to ensure consistency

● a core curriculum to clarify what learners should know to reach those standards

● a new system of qualifications to measure achievements against the standards

● improved quality and diversity of learning opportunities to meet the needs of a wide range of learners.

The standards describe adult literacy as 'the ability ... to read, write and speak in English... at a level necessary to function at work and in society in general'.

The standards provide a map of the range of skills that you are expected to need.

Literacy covers the ability to:

● speak, listen and respond

● read and comprehend

● write to communicate.

Level 2 of the national adult literacy standards is equivalent to Key Skills Level 2 and NVQ Level 2.

How is adult literacy assessed?

To gain the Certificate in Adult Literacy at Level 2 you will need to pass a test. The test lasts for 1 hour. It is a multiple-choice test. This means that you will be given four possible answers to each question and you will have to pick the right answer. You will not have to write out any answers. You mark the right answer on the answer sheet.

Entering for the test

You can take the test for the Certificate in Adult Literacy at various times of the year. (Ask your nearest test centre for details and exact times.)

If you have been working through this course with a tutor, ask your tutor if they can arrange for you to take the Certificate in Adult Literacy Level 2.

If you have been working through this course alone, you will have to contact a test centre to arrange to take the test for the Certificate. Most Colleges of Further Education are test centres. If you are also working towards an NVQ or other qualification, your training provider may be able to help you to arrange to take the test. If you need more help in finding a test centre you can phone **learndirect** on 0800 100 900. They will be able to give you details about centres near you.

You need to make sure you register for the test in plenty of time; some centres will need you to register two months before the test date. You may be charged a fee to take the test. You will need to ask the centre about this when you register.

Section 1: Ways to read

Section 1: Ways to read

This first section looks at different ways of reading. There are many different ways of reading. How you read will depend on:

- **the level at which you are working**

  For example, a long, complicated technical report will take more time and effort to read than a short note from a friend. The level at which you are working will be shown by:

  - ✗ how difficult the language is to read
  - ✗ the length of the material.

- **what you need from what you are reading**

  This can range from reading a novel for pleasure to reading a technical report for information.

- **the material you are reading**

  For example, there are big differences between how we read newspapers and how we read letters from a bank manager or a solicitor.

Topic 1: How can I get information from written material?

How you get information from written material will depend on what you are doing. If you are reading at work, for example, you will probably be pushed for time. Essays in education have to be written to a deadline. Newspapers and novels, on the other hand, can be read at your own speed.

Reasons for completing this topic

This topic will help you to:

- think about what you read
- understand why you read
- look at your own ways of reading.

Why do *you* read?

Start by thinking about why you read. Try Activity 1.

Activity 1

Write down five things you have read in the past couple of weeks and say why you read them. You can include all kinds of things, not just books and newspapers. Include both short and long pieces of writing if you can.

What I have read	Why I read it
1	
2	
3	
4	
5	

Now look at our suggestions opposite. Your list will be different, but some of the reasons behind your answers will be the same.

Suggestions for Activity 1

Did you have any of the following?

What I have read	Why I read it
1 Novel	For pleasure
2 Teletext	Information – football scores
3 Newspaper	Information – news
4 Newspaper	For pleasure – crossword
5 Leaflet on smoking	Information – practice nurse gave it to me and asked me to read it
6 Rail timetable	Information – to plan journey
7 Note from partner	Information – s/he wanted me to take the cat to the vet
8 Internet article on healthy eating	Information – trying to lose weight
9 Report on adult reading	Information – writing essay on adult reading
10 Cereal packet	Information – trying to eat healthy diet and wanted to know what was in the cereal

You can see how many different types of texts we read and the different reasons for reading them. This is the idea of *reading for a purpose*. Keep this in mind when you are working through the rest of the module.

Reflective learning log

Make a note in your learning log of your main reasons for reading. It is worth returning to this as you work through this module, especially if you begin to lose sight of your reasons for doing the course.

Being an active reader

Is it worthwhile reading something when time is short? The answer is that it can be, but you must decide whether or not you are going to read something *before* you start. If you do this, you are being an **active reader**.

Spending time thinking about material before reading it is an important first step in improving how you read it. With help from this module and plenty of practice, you should find that you can make decisions about what you want to read quickly and effectively. This will save you time and effort.

Active readers ask themselves the following questions before they start reading.

Questions to ask before reading

● Will I look at the material?

   Does it contain information that I need or should I look at another source?

   Does it look good from the outside?

   Does the cover tell me anything?

   Is it a proper report?

● Why should I read it?

   Does it cover what I want?

   Can I understand the words or are they too difficult?

   Is it at my level?

● How much time can I afford to spend reading it?

   What other things do I have to do?

   What will I get out of reading it?

   Will I be disadvantaged if I don't read it?

Hint
Try to be an active reader every time you read something. This means thinking *before* you read.

Active reading is linked with **scanning**. You will look at this in the next topic.

Now try Activity 2, which should help you to assess how well you are doing as an active reader.

Activity 2

> Over the next week or so keep a diary of what you read and make a note of why you read it. Also keep a note of how long you spent on each piece of reading and how effective your reading was.
>
> Use these headings for your diary, if you want to.
>
> **Day/date**
>
> **What I read**
>
> **Why I read it**
>
> **How long I spent reading it**
>
> **How effective my reading was (how much I got out of it)**
>
> **Any problems I had with it (e.g. new words, meanings)**

Hint

This activity requires you to keep a diary over a fairly long period. Start it *now* and make a note somewhere to remind yourself to fill it in each day.

Suggestions for Activity 2

Your diary should give you some idea of how your reading is improving. Look for signs like these.

● Do I read more quickly?

● Do I have to use a dictionary less often?

● Is my understanding of what I read better?

● Do I understand more difficult language?

Everyone has a different way of reading, but here are the reflections of one person who has really worked on his reading skills:

1 The speed of my reading has improved with practice over the years.

2 I find I read better:

● early in the morning

● when I have everything in front of me that I am going to need so I do not have to stop to find a highlighter pen or a clean sheet of paper

● when I take a break after an hour of reading

● when I enjoy what I am reading

● when I have a target before I start, e.g. to write an essay.

3 I still find technical writing difficult to read.

Reflective learning log

Make a note of anything your diary has revealed to you about your reading skills and habits. Return to this every so often as you work through the module and make a note of any further progress you have made in your reading skills.

Summary

In this first topic you have thought about what you read and why you read it. You have looked at your own ways of reading and you may have identified some of the problems you have with certain kinds of reading.

> By completing Topic 1 you have covered point 5 of the 'Text Focus' section of the Adult Literacy Core Curriculum. It has also been an introduction to identifying the purpose of texts (point 2).

Topic 2: What are the different ways of reading?

In this topic you will be looking at the main ways of reading:

- scanning
- skimming
- reading in depth
- reading critically.

Reasons for completing this topic

This topic will help you to:

- use different ways of reading to find information
- speed up your reading
- make your reading more efficient.

When do we use scanning?

We use **scanning** to help us decide if something is going to be worth reading.

Scanning helps us decide:

- will I open it?
- will I read it?
- how much time will I spend reading it?

This saves time if we want to read a lot of text.

Scanning is not just for information texts. We can also scan to decide if a novel is worth buying or borrowing from a library.

Now try Activity 3.

Activity 3

1 Think of the last time you bought or borrowed a book to read for pleasure. Write down below some thoughts on why you chose that book.

2 Have you bought any magazines or newspapers in the last few months? Jot down in the space below some ideas about what made you buy them.

Suggestions for Activity 3

Here are some ideas for why you might choose books, magazines or newspapers. Don't worry if your ideas aren't the same as these.

Books

Description of the book on the back cover.

I had already read and liked something by the same writer.

The pictures/illustrations on the front cover.

It was recommended by a friend.

I read a good review of the book.

I read the first paragraph of the first chapter and liked what I read.

I saw the film of the book.

Magazines and newspapers

The magazine covers my special interest, mountain biking.

The newspaper has a motoring section and I wanted to find out prices for second-hand cars.

I enjoyed reading the magazine in the hairdressers.

I like the newspaper crossword.

Again, what you have written will depend on your own tastes and habits. I buy both newspapers and magazines without really looking at what is inside. I may scan the contents page of a magazine, but I rarely look at a newspaper before buying it.

Reflective learning log

Write down notes on:

● what makes certain publications unattractive to you

● publications you would deliberately never buy.

Send the notes to your tutor with the first assignment.

Now think about reference books and textbooks.

Activity 4

1   Think of a reference book or textbook that you have used. (This could include the Yellow Pages, a local telephone directory, a television programmes listing magazine.) How did you decide if it was going to be useful? Were you right? Was it useful? What made it useful? Write your thoughts down below.

2   Write down the parts of a reference book or textbook you think could be scanned quickly to see if it is going to be any use.

Suggestions for Activity 4

The way you choose reference books and textbooks is probably not the same as the way you choose novels, magazines or newspapers. I would spend some time making sure it was the right book. To read a reference book or textbook is going to take a lot of my time and I have to be sure that it will be worth the effort.

> **Hint**
> Look at the book before you read it.

I would scan the:

- title

- back cover

- date of publication

- contents page

- chapter headings

- any sub-headings

- summaries at the end of a chapter

- first paragraph of a chapter

- last paragraph of a chapter.

When do we use skimming?

Skimming means reading a text quickly to get the main points.

Skimming help us to:

- preview material before we read it in detail

- check if we understand something after we have read it carefully.

The next three activities will help you to practise your skimming skills.

Activity 5

1   Using a watch or timer to check yourself, take 15 seconds only to read the leaflet below. Then cover it with a piece of paper and answer the questions below.

Help with English and Maths can improve

Confidence with Money
Booking holidays
Reading to Children
Learning to drive
Using reference books
Completing forms
Social Skills
Using the Internet

All Basic Skills courses are free
Contact Aisha on 01234 56789

---

a)   What is the cost of Basic Skills courses?

b)   Who should you contact?

c)   Write three things that 'Help with English and Maths' can improve.

d)   What is Aisha's phone number?

2   How easy did you find this activity? What things about the leaflet made it hard or easy to read? Note down your ideas below.

Activity 5 continued

3   Using your watch or a timer, take 5 seconds to re-read the leaflet, cover it and answer the same questions again below.

a)   What is the cost of Basic Skills courses?

b)   Who should you contact?

c)   Write three things that 'Help with English and Maths' can improve.

d)   What is Aisha's phone number?

Suggestions for Activity 5

The first part of the activity is to practise reading quickly just to get the main ideas. Your answers should be like these.

1   a)   Basic Skills courses are free.

b)   Aisha

c)   Any three from the following:

● your confidence in dealing with money

● booking holidays

● reading to children

● learning to drive

● using reference books

● completing forms

● social skills

● using the Internet.

d)   Aisha's phone number is 01234 56789.

You might have found this activity fairly easy first time round because the leaflet is laid out well. There are clear headings, bold titles and plenty of space between the lines. You were probably able to pick out the main points.

You should have done even better the second time. By this time, you knew what the questions were going to be, so you were reading for a purpose. This should have helped you to concentrate and come up with your answers more quickly.

The next activity is similar to Activity 5. It is longer, but will help you to practise the same skills of reading for a purpose.

Activity 6

The following text is taken from a careers guidance leaflet.

1   Using your watch or a timer, read through it in no more than 5 minutes.

Then cover it and answer the questions below.

> Many parents who have taken time off work while their children are small are worried that when they go back to work their whole world will change, often for the worse. The information in this leaflet contains help and advice for anyone who is returning to work after having a family.
>
> Confidential advice is also available through a personal interview.
>
> **WHAT CAN YOU DO TO PREPARE YOURSELF TO GO BACK TO WORK?**
>
> There are a number of courses available in local further education colleges in your area where you can either learn new things or brush up on the talents you already have. Getting qualifications in computing is particularly useful and there are a number of other courses specifically designed for the adult returner.
>
> **DOES YOUR CONFIDENCE NEED A BOOST?**
>
> Most people who have been away from paid work for a while lack self-confidence. Try going back to education or other training and you will find that meeting people will help you believe in yourself again.
>
> **WHAT TYPE OF WORK? WHAT TYPE OF JOB?**
>
> You may find that voluntary work is what you want at first, or you may wish to go straight back to paid work.
>
> Many jobs can be done on a part-time basis and job sharing may be a possibility.
>
> You will need to think about the sort of work you can do and how to fit it in with your other responsibilities.

a)   Where are courses available?

Activity 6 continued

b)   How is confidential advice available?

c)   What kind of work might people want?

d)   At whom is the leaflet aimed?

e)   How do you know?

Hint
Think about layout and language. Look for headings, capital letters and paragraphs.

f)   Do you think the leaflet is well written? Can you think of any ways of improving it?

2   Re-read the leaflet, cover it and answer the same questions. Make a note of how long it took to read this time.

a)   Where are courses available?

b)   How is confidential advice available?

c)   What kind of work might people want?

d)   At whom is the leaflet aimed?

e)   How do you know?

f)   Do you think the leaflet is well written? Can you think of any ways of improving it?

Suggestions for Activity 6

Here are some ideas. Your answers may have been slightly different.

a)   local Further Education Colleges

b)   through a personal interview

c)   voluntary or paid

d)   The leaflet is aimed at parents:

- who gave up work to have children and are thinking of returning to education or work

- who are not confident about going back to work.

e)   Because it says it in the first paragraph. Also, the heading 'DOES YOUR CONFIDENCE NEED A BOOST?'gives us a clue.

f)   I think the leaflet is easy to read because it has clear, simple words.

I think it could have been improved because:

✗   there is too much writing

✗   the headings would have been easier to read if they had been in bold or italics rather than capitals

✗   there is no title, so you have to read all of it to find out what it is about.

It should have been easier to read the second time because you knew what you were looking for. You probably read it more quickly and answered more questions correctly. This is because you were reading for a purpose.

Activity 7 will give you the chance to practise on the type of text that is common to see at work.

Hint

Know what you want before you start to read.

Activity 7

1   Read the following passage quickly, cover it and answer the
    questions that follow.

MEMORANDUM   **LOGOTRON**.com

From: Patrick Scott (Managing Director)

To: The Health and Safety Officer

Reference: Your memorandum

Date: 8 November

Thank you for your memorandum on the letter the
Company has received from the Health and Safety
Executive.

I would like you to write a letter to the Health and
Safety Executive giving the following information:

1   We have no written Health and Safety Policy, but
    will have one ready by July.

2   All staff have been trained in Health and Safety and
    every member of staff holds a First Aid Certificate.

The Company sees the following as its two main areas
of concern for health and safety:

● lack of no-smoking policy

● staff removing guards from their machines.

---

a)   What is the name of the Managing Director?

b)   What is the date of the memorandum?

c)   What information does the Managing Director want the
     Health and Safety Officer to give to the Health and
     Safety Executive?

d)   What are the two areas of concern for health and
     safety?

2   Now check your answers by re-reading the memo. How did
    you do?

Suggestions for Activity 7

If you answered all the questions right you did very well. Most people would not have taken in all the information at once and would have to re-read the text with the questions in mind.

If you want to practise writing memos, try Section 1 of the 'Writing' module.

Reflective learning log

Make a note in your learning log of:

● different ways you have been reading while doing the previous activities, e.g. fast, carefully

● ways in which you think you have improved your reading skills.

Return them to your tutor with the assignment for this section.

Scanning and skimming will only give you a broad outline of a text. To get more information you need to read in depth. You will be looking at this next.

Reading in depth

Reading in depth means reading something carefully to get accurate information. You usually do this when you are reading long or complicated material such as books or reports.

We have seen how skimming and scanning can help you decide:

● how useful a text is going to be

● how much time you need to spend on it.

To understand a text fully, however, you now have to read it a lot more carefully. This does not mean that you have to read every word in the text or that you have to read slowly – the secret is to read *efficiently*.

Reflective learning log

Make notes on how you have felt in the past if you have needed to read long texts. Think about what special difficulties you faced. In the light of what you have done and read so far in this section what would you have done differently?

Hint
BE AN ACTIVE
READER.

People who are not used to *reading for a purpose* often read phrases or passages several times because they have not fully understood them the first time.

Re-reading a passage a lot of times will not make you a good reader.

It is more important that you set up a *rhythm of reading* which lets you read smoothly – if you come across a difficult phrase or passage carry on but make a note in your mind that you may have to come back later.

The same applies to difficult or unfamiliar words – always stopping to use a dictionary will not make you an efficient reader.

Keep a note in your mind of where the difficult or unfamiliar word was and go back to it after you have finished reading the whole document.

Activity 8

Read the following passage.

1   As you are reading, **don't stop** if you come across a word or phrase that you don't understand, but make a note in your mind to go back to it after you have finished the whole thing.

2   When you have finished, read the passage again and see if it makes sense to you.

3   Now look in the dictionary and write down the meanings of the words or phrases that you didn't understand.

Hint
Keep going!

There is no official requirement as to the number of first aiders to workers so employers tend to have no fixed policy about the number of first aiders they need in their company.

The reluctance of employers to have a fixed policy is financial. Companies are reluctant to take on something that could cost them a great deal of money in the long run. The number of persons who need to be trained as first aiders should depend on the size of the company and what it produces. A small office will only need one first aider, while a large factory will need more.

Employees also need to realise that they have a duty to keep the workplace safe. They must all work together to keep the work environment safe and be constantly reminding their colleagues that they need to know about health and safety.

Suggestions for Activity 8

You should have gained some idea of the meaning of the passage from the first reading, but there were not many clues as to what it was about. This was because it didn't have any:

● titles

● sub-headings

● highlighting

to give you guidance and show you which parts of the passage were most important.

If you used a dictionary you probably found it stopped you from getting into a rhythm of reading.

When I tried this exercise I found the words 'reluctance' and 'environment' difficult. I needed to look them up in the dictionary. This took time and the definitions I found didn't really fit into the passage.

The next activity will give you more practice on reading efficiently and in depth.

Activity 9

Hint
Look closely at signs the writer is giving you to show which parts of the passage are more important than others

Read the following passage. Don't stop if you find any words or phrases difficult. Then cover the passage and answer the questions that follow.

HEALTH AND SAFETY: ERECTION OF SIGNS

Under the Health and Safety (Safety Signs and Signals) Regulations the *employer* has to identify hazards in the workplace and erect signs to warn of possible dangers. These signs will use as few words as possible and all posters and displays will contain *colour and pictures*.

Health and safety is everyone's responsibility

We cannot stress enough that it is the responsibility of *all* in the workplace to improve health and safety. Everybody needs to be aware that it is part of their everyday job to work safely. Remember health and safety is not just about signs and posters but also about how *everyone* should behave.

---

1   Who has the job of identifying hazards in the workplace?

2   How many words must the signs have?

3   What should posters and displays contain?

4   Who has the responsibility for meeting health and safety standards?

Suggestions for Activity 9

You should have found this passage easier to read in depth because:

- the text was probably not as difficult as that in the previous activities

- **bold** headings and *italics* gave you a lot more guidance on what the writer felt was important.

The answers are:

1   the employer

2   as few as possible

3   colour and pictures

4   everyone in the workplace.

Reflective learning log

Make a note of the differences in your reading between Activities 5 and 9. Did your speed improve? Did you find information more quickly? Do you think there are any improvements in how you are reading?

Hint
Remember what we have said about scanning and skimming.

What do I need to do to improve my reading in depth?

When you are reading it is important that you get *actively involved* with the text.

This is how you do it.

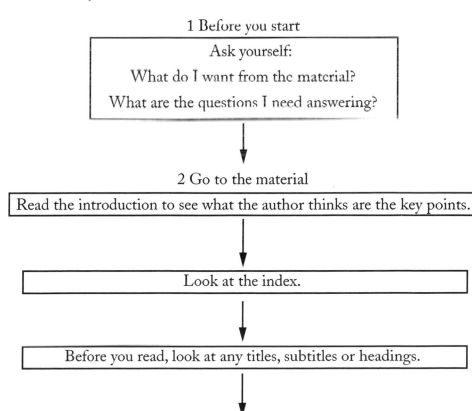

1 Before you start

Ask yourself:

What do I want from the material?

What are the questions I need answering?

2 Go to the material

Read the introduction to see what the author thinks are the key points.

Look at the index.

Before you read, look at any titles, subtitles or headings.

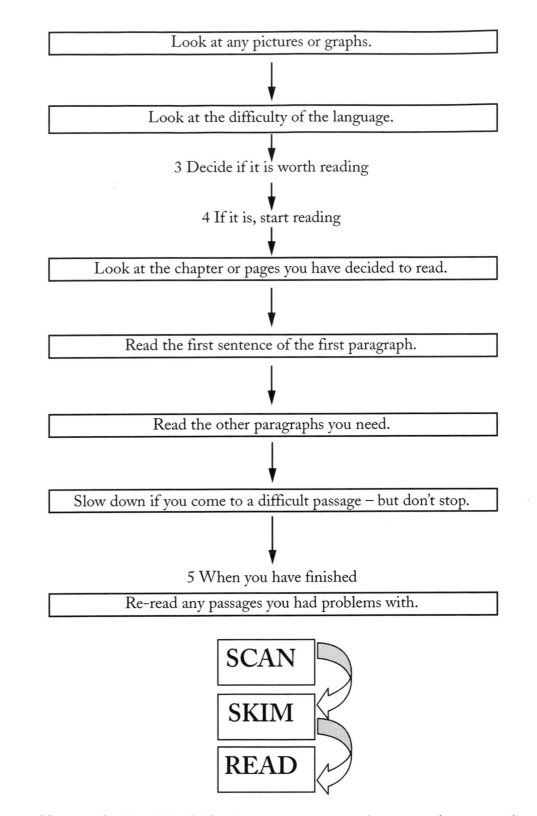

| Look at any pictures or graphs. |

↓

| Look at the difficulty of the language. |

↓

3 Decide if it is worth reading

↓

4 If it is, start reading

↓

| Look at the chapter or pages you have decided to read. |

↓

| Read the first sentence of the first paragraph. |

↓

| Read the other paragraphs you need. |

↓

| Slow down if you come to a difficult passage – but don't stop. |

↓

5 When you have finished

| Re-read any passages you had problems with. |

SCAN
SKIM
READ

Now try Activity 10, which gives you an opportunity to practise your active reading.

Activity 10

Read the following passage, which has been adapted from a holiday brochure. After you have read the passage, you will be asked questions about:

● where the holiday centres are

● what types of activities are available

● the cost of the brochure.

GoFar Trails

Your holiday prayers answered

If you are looking for a peaceful and relaxing holiday then look no further than GoFar Trails. From small beginnings five years ago when the company had only one location, we are now able to offer a range of six completely different locations. Whatever your idea of a perfect holiday we have the answer.

The beauty of our holidays is that they are designed with you in mind. You tell us what you want and we will do our best to get it for you.

If the idea of an activity holiday appeals to you we have a range of land- or sea-based activities for you.

We have centres in Northumberland, Scotland and Wales and can arrange walking holidays. Walk across England or America and we will arrange all accommodation and food requirements.

On the other hand, if your idea of a great holiday is to chill out by the pool under a hot sun abroad, we again have the answer. We have centres in Italy, Greece and Spain. If you are feeling more adventurous we can arrange holidays in Africa or the Far East.

Our prices are very reasonable and are highly recommended by *Which? Magazine* and a number of television holiday programmes.

Send now for a free brochure but hurry as we fill up quickly!

1   How many centres are available?

2   Where are they located?

3   Which centres are abroad?

4   How much does the brochure cost?

Suggestions for Activity 10

This time you knew which questions were going to be asked and read the passage with these in mind. This should have made the activity easier as you were reading with a purpose.

The answers are:

1   Six

2   Northumberland, Scotland, Wales, Italy, Greece and Spain.

3   The centres in Italy, Greece and Spain.

4   Nothing – it is a free brochure.

Reading critically

Reading critically means never accepting written material without asking questions. For example, does a report contain all the information needed and is it written clearly so that people can understand it?

Once you have started to read critically, you will be well on the way to being a *good* reader rather than just a reader.

Summary

In Topic 2 you have looked at how you can get information from written material, including scanning, skimming and reading in depth. Don't worry if you have not fully understood the ideas, particularly on what to do to improve your reading in depth. We will return to reading in depth later and you will be given plenty of practice!

Self-check 1

Hint
Some may include more than one method.

Try the following to check that you have understood the main ideas from Section 1.

1   Write down what you understand by scanning, skimming, reading in depth and give one or two ideas of when you would use each.

Way of reading	What it means	When I would use it
Scanning		
Skimming		
Reading in depth		

2   Write in the method of reading you would use for the following:

Deciding whether or not to
buy a book from a bookshop

Summarising a report for
your boss

Reading your gas bill

Reading a hire purchase
agreement

Checking a bus timetable

Finding a suitable holiday
in a travel brochure

Finding a station on a map
of the London Underground

A novel

A newspaper

A company newsletter

Answers to these self-check exercises are at the end of the section.

By completing Topic 2 you have used different reading strategies to find information and so have covered point 7 of the 'Text Focus' section of the Adult Literacy Core Curriculum. It has also been an introduction to identifying the main points of texts (point 2) and grammar and punctuation ('Sentence Focus' 1 and 2).

Reflective learning log

Make a note of some of the things you have learned from the two topics in Section 1. Write down anything about your reading that you think has improved as a result of working through this section. As you work through the rest of the module try to make a note in your learning log if you use the things you have learned in this section.

Section summary

This section is long because the skills we cover are such an important part of your becoming a *GOOD* reader. The section was designed to speed up your reading but at the same time improve the quality of what you get from material. The skills you have learnt need to be practiced – now use them on everything you read!

Suggestions for Self-check 1

Here are our suggestions. How do they compare with your responses? If yours are very different, you should look through Section 1 again.

1

Way of reading	What it means	When I would use it
Scanning	Looking through a text very quickly, to find information by locating a key word.	When looking at a book and deciding if it is going to be worth reading.
Skimming	Reading a text quickly to get the main points.	To preview material to get before reading it in detail or to check that I understand something after reading it.
Reading in depth	Reading something carefully to get accurate information.	I usually do this when I am reading long or complicated material such as books or reports.

2

Deciding whether or not to buy a book from a bookshop	scanning/skimming
Summarising a report for your boss	intensive
Reading your gas bill	scanning; maybe reading in depth
Reading a hire purchase agreement	reading in depth
Checking a bus timetable	scanning
Finding a suitable holiday in a travel brochure	scanning
Finding a station on a map of the London Underground	skimming
A novel	reading in depth
A newspaper	scanning/skimming
A company newsletter	scanning

Section 2: Reading different types of text

Section 2: Reading different types of text

Welcome to Section 2. This section looks at reading different types of text.

It is important to be able to recognise that people write things for different reasons. For example, someone writing for a newspaper might be trying to entertain or inform people and encourage them to buy that newspaper. Someone writing a do-it-yourself manual will want to write as clearly and simply as possible so that people can easily follow the instructions. If we can recognise what a piece of writing is trying to say quickly, we can make quick decisions on how we are going to approach it. If a do-it-yourself manual, for example, has too much writing and no pictures it is not likely to be of much use – so we can decide quickly to look for a better version.

In this section you will be looking at different types of written material – or texts – and how to recognise them from their:

● audience

● purpose

● language and layout.

You will also be looking at the difference between **formal** and **informal** texts.

Topic 1: Looking at different kinds of texts

Before we can talk about 'texts' we need to know what texts are. Texts are any kind of written material. Texts can range from a letter to a friend to a complicated government report; from a very long novel like *War and Peace*, to a note to the milkman cancelling the milk.

Reasons for completing this topic

This topic will help you to:

● understand that different types of writing are meant to do different things

● see that the way a text is written can give clues to its real meaning.

Different kinds of text

Many of us see text in a newspaper every day. The text in a newspaper is made up of sections, stories, headlines and pictures. It includes:

● articles of different length

● advertisements

● regular features such as the weather report, television programmes, horoscopes

● one-off articles.

Another kind of text is a **novel,** which is longer and usually has chapters. Texts can also be very short. A **text message** on a mobile phone or an **email** are both texts which give information or send a greeting.

How to tell?

To decide which kind of text you are dealing with you have to look for clues. Here are some ideas.

● Who is it aimed at (who is the **audience**)? For example, is the writing aimed at people who might have similar ideas to the author? Or is the author trying to get people to change their way of thinking?

● How is it written? Is it long? Is it short? Does it have paragraphs? Does it have pictures?

● Is it laid out in a formal way with headings, bullet points etc., or is it written just to be attractive to the reader?

● What type of language is used? Is it formal or informal? Are long or complicated words used?

● What is the writer – or **author** – trying to do? Is it to:

   – inform

   – instruct

   – persuade

   – amuse?

There is more on the difference between formal and informal text in the next topic.

You will be thinking about different kinds of text in this activity.

Activity 1

Think of six different kinds of text and fill in the table. Try to fill in each of the columns:

- audience – who the text is aimed at
- purpose – why the text has been written
- language and layout – key features of how the text is written and set out.

The first row has been completed to give you some ideas.

Hint

Some texts may have more than one purpose and/or more than one audience.

Type of text	Audience	Purpose	Language and layout
Birthday card	Person whose birthday it is	To show you have remembered their birthday and wish them well	Short message, informal
1			
2			
3			
4			
5			
6			

Read through the following suggestions, before continuing.

Suggestions for Activity 1

You will have your own ideas, but here are some suggestions. As you will see from the suggestions, every text has an audience and purpose, and a certain kind of language and layout. All these features can help you tell what kind of text it is, although some features are shared by more than one kind of text.

Type of text	Audience	Purpose	Language and layout
Birthday card	Person whose birthday it is	To show you have remembered their birthday and wish them well	Short message, informal
1 Newspaper article on mortgages	General public	To give information about different kinds of mortgage scheme	Headline, picture, short paragraphs
2 Health and safety memo	Company employees	To give up to date information on health and safety regulations	Short, simple, headings and pictures
3 Parish magazine	Residents of parish	To inform and entertain people in parish	Short articles, advertisements, diary
4 Mobile phone text message	Receiver of text message	To give information or a greeting	Very short words, abbreviations, text message symbols
5 Novel	Novel readers	To entertain	Chapters, may be complex words and sentences, may be some pictures
6 Specialist magazine	Specialist readers	To inform and/or entertain	Index, articles, letters, pictures, advertisements
7 Handwritten note to traffic warden	Traffic warden	To give information	Short, simple message
8 Email message	One person or several people if copied	To send information or a greeting	Short, simple words and sentences, abbreviations
9 Textbook for GCSE students	GCSE students	To give information and aid learning	Contents page, chapters, different sections, pictures, index

Cross-reference

You will find more on style of language (formal/informal), different kinds of writing and different audiences in Section 1 of the 'Writing' module.

Reflective learning log

Make notes on the audience, purpose, language and layout of anything you may have written recently.

Layout and style

Different kinds of text have different kinds of layout and style. For example a *formal report* should contain:

● bullet points

● lots of headings

● **bold** and *italicised* writing.

A *Valentine card*, however, would be sent to show affection. The text is usually a short caring or amusing message with pictures on the Valentine theme.

A **poster** usually contains:

● lots of colour

● as few words as possible

● attention-grabbing words such as FREE or NEW.

Emails are short and may contain abbreviations.

Activity 2

1   List below the features of language or layout you would expect to see in the following types of text. For each one, try to say why you think the text has these features.

Type of text	Features of language or layout	Why it has these features
a) article from a tabloid newspaper on foot and mouth disease		
b) a government report on foot and mouth disease		

Activity 2 continued

c) a poster informing people of the precautions they need to take to avoid foot and mouth disease when walking in the countryside

2   Highlight the key features that distinguish each kind of text from the other kinds.

Suggestions for Activity 2

Here are our suggestions. We have underlined the key features that make the types of text different. As you can see, these features are usually to do with the *audience* at which the texts are aimed and the *messages* they are trying to pass on.

Type of text	Features of language or layout	Why it has these features
a) article from a tabloid newspaper on foot and mouth disease	<u>Simple</u> language <u>Sensational</u> language <u>Short</u> paragraphs <u>Short</u> words **Biased** language <u>Photographs</u> <u>Quotes</u> from farmers	This kind of text has to provide information to its readers, but at the same time keep their interest, as their target is to increase the number of people buying the newspaper.
b) a government report on foot and mouth disease	Introductory <u>summary</u> <u>Longer</u> words More <u>formal</u> language Headings <u>No pictures</u> but probably other images such as <u>graphs or tables</u> <u>References</u> <u>Appendices</u> <u>Separate conclusions</u>	This kind of text is aimed at experts in the subject or people who are able to judge the truth or otherwise of the information that is included. However, the information included may only support the Government's case. Information that is *not* included could also be significant.

Type of text	Features of language or layout	Why it has these features
c) a poster informing people of the precautions they need to take to avoid foot and mouth disease when walking in the countryside	<u>Simple</u> language <u>Limited number</u> of words <u>Key</u> words <u>Colour</u> <u>Pictures</u>	This text has one job – to pass on a message to the general public quickly and efficiently. It needs to attract people's attention though not necessarily for any length of time. Colour, pictures and key words are used to make the poster attractive and easy to understand.

Reflective learning log

Make notes on an advertisement you have read recently stating what the key features of the language and layout were. Why did you choose that advertisement to look at rather than any other?

Summary

In Topic 1 you have looked at different kinds of texts and the key features of each kind.

> By completing this topic you have covered point 1 of the 'Text Focus' section of the Adult Literacy Core Curriculum: 'trace and understand the main events of continuous descriptive, explanatory and persuasive texts'. The topic also covers 'Text Focus' point 2 and grammar and punctuation ('Sentence Focus' points 1 and 2).

Topic 2: Reading formal and informal texts

You have now looked at different kinds of text. This second topic focuses on the differences between formal and informal texts.

Reasons for completing this topic

This topic will help you to:

● see differences between formal and informal writing

● compare information from different sources.

Formal texts

Formal texts are usually written to pass on messages or information. They are set out in a formal style with formal language. For example, a formal document might have phrases such as 'We are writing to express our concern that...' and 'We feel it is important that...', whereas in an informal letter to a friend you would include phrases such as 'How are you?' or 'Hope you're keeping well.', or 'Sorry not to have been in touch.'

Informal texts

Informal texts will have simple, easy-to-understand language and may have pictures and colours.

Cross-reference

If you want to find out more about the differences between formal and informal writing, turn to Section 1 of the 'Writing' module.

Reflective learning log

Make some notes on the differences between a letter you would write to a friend and a letter you would write to an insurance company. Think mainly about the language and layout.

Also think about differences in language you would use if you were talking to a friend and someone from an insurance company.

Activity 3

Hint
Think about the people it is aimed at and what the texts are trying to do.

Tick the column you think describes these different kinds of text.

Type of text	Formal	Informal
letter from a solicitor		
poster advertising a circus		
community group newsletter		
government report on foot and mouth disease		
article in the sports section of a tabloid newspaper		
letter of complaint to a railway company		
local government guide to planning applications		
company health and safety report		
birthday card		
novel		
health and safety leaflet for employees		
hire purchase agreement document		

Suggestions for Activity 3

It should have been easy to decide on some of these. For example, a letter from a solicitor is always formal. Legal letters are full of long words and complicated phrases. Posters and greetings cards are meant to persuade or amuse people so will have simple messages, pictures and plenty of colour. Formal documents are meant to be accurate and to inform, so very precise language is necessary.

Some texts are more difficult to categorise. For example, a health and safety leaflet is about a formal topic, but as it is meant to get a message across to the employees it is likely to be laid out in an informal fashion with simple language, plenty of colour, and perhaps some pictures.

A letter of complaint is also formal, but the language used must not be so complicated that the message is unclear.

Here are our ideas.

Type of text	Formal	Informal
letter from a solicitor	✓	
poster advertising a circus		✓
community group newsletter		✓
government report on foot and mouth disease	✓	
article in the sports section of a tabloid newspaper		✓
letter of complaint to a railway company	✓	
local government guide to planning applications	✓	
company health and safety report	✓	
birthday card		✓
novel		✓
health and safety leaflet for employees		✓
hire purchase agreement document	✓	

Reflective learning log

Make a list of any formal or informal letters you have received in the past month. Write down any differences you have noticed between them.

Categories of text

Written material can be **explanatory, persuasive** or **descriptive**. Some texts fall into more than one category. Look again at the introduction to Section 2 to see why we need to know what type a text is.

Explanatory texts

Explanatory texts explain how and why something happens or happened. Good explanatory texts are written in a simple, logical style and include a number of helpful features such as graphs, charts, bullet points and numbered headings. An example of an explanatory text is an instruction manual.

Activity 4

1   Read the following passage and think about what features make it an explanatory text.

INSTRUCTIONS FOR USE OF A TRIANGULAR BANDAGE

Ask the casualty to sit down and support the injured limb. Place the forearm across the chest with the fingertips resting on the opposite shoulder. Place an open bandage over the forearm and hand with its point along the elbow. Still supporting the forearm ease the base of the bandage around the hand, forearm and elbow. Carry the power end across the back and over to the front of the uninjured shoulder. Gently adjust the height of the sling if necessary and using a reef knot tie off the sound side in front of the hollow above the collarbone.

2   What changes could be made to make it more effective as an explanatory text? Make a note of your ideas below.

Hint
Think about the layout.

Suggestions for Activity 4

This is an explanatory text because it is explaining how to do something. It gives instructions. I don't think this is very effective as an explanatory text. It could have been improved by:

● pictures to illustrate the points

● separating the points and listing them with numbers or bullets.

You might have had some other ideas.

Activity 5

Read the following passage and think about what features make it a descriptive text.

ROVERS FIND A NEW HOME AT LAST

Doncaster Rovers have finally been given the green light for their new £8 million stadium.

The often bitter battle with local councillors ended last night when Doncaster Council earmarked £1 million for a study on a 10,000-capacity complex in the town's prestigious Lakeside area.

Rovers hope the Stadium will be ready by 2004 and plan to share with Doncaster Dragons and Doncaster Belles Ladies Football Club.

Suggestions for Activity 5

The story is just giving an account of an event that has taken place. The language used is trying to get over facts, rather than an argument or instructions.

Persuasive texts

Persuasive texts are texts that try to persuade the reader. They normally have:

● a point of view

● arguments and evidence to support that point of view.

Some persuasive texts such as advertisements use simple words and bright pictures to persuade people. Try the next activity, which looks at whether or not texts are persuasive.

Activity 6

Study the following texts. How would you say they try to persuade the reader?

How does it try to persuade the reader?

Text 1

Text 2

Text 3

Text 1

SALE

TOTAL CARPET MADNESS
means an amazing 40% off most marked carpet
and vinyl prices. You would be mad to miss it!
MUST END WEDNESDAY!

Text 2

But perhaps the best guarantee of all is that in 40 years of specialising in outdoor play, every toy we make passes the toughest test of all — our own children. Only if their faces light up does it get the thumbs up, ensuring that Tougher Toys really are the best by smiles.

Text 3

To the Editor

Dear Sir

The number of cars dumped in the city is now beyond a joke. It is absolutely horrendous that no one is taking an interest in something which is causing such a danger to our children.

The situation needs to be tackled NOW, not tomorrow. If nothing is done quickly someone will be killed and our Town Councillors will have blood on their hands.

Yours not very faithfully

Anne Angry

Suggestions for Activity 6

Here are some ideas. You should have spotted different layouts and language to explanatory and descriptive texts. These texts are trying to *persuade* the reader.

Here are our ideas.

	How does it try to persuade the reader?
Text 1	● Words like 'madness', 'amazing' and 'mad' to grab your attention and make you read the advertisement. Words like these are called emotive words. Although they are attention grabbing, they do not really give any information and often exaggerate. ● Bold type and capitals to emphasise. ● Phrase 'Must end Wednesday' suggests you have to hurry to take advantage of the offer.
Text 2	● Appeals to parents by using the ideas of children and safety together. Uses 'our own children'. ● Also uses the word 'smiles instead of 'miles' to add humour. ● Plays on the idea that good parents would only buy their children safe toys. ● Suggests that only their toys will make children smile.
Text 3	● Language used is extreme – 'horrendous', 'killed', 'blood on their hands' – and emotive. ● Highlights the safety of children. ● Play on words at the end – 'Yours not very faithfully' rather than 'Yours faithfully' makes you read it twice. ● No attempt to be fair or quote opposite points of view.

Descriptive texts

Descriptive texts describe people or events without passing judgement on them or offering an explanation.

Activity 7

Hints

1 Look up the meanings of 'explanatory', 'persuasive' and 'descriptive' in the Glossary.

2 Some of the texts could fall into more than one category.

Decide which category each of these texts is and tick the column.

Type of text	Explanatory	Persuasive	Descriptive
DIY manual			
guide to a museum			
letter to a local newspaper arguing the case for foxhunting			
instructions for operating a DVD player			
newspaper report of a football match			
booklet with details of the services offered by a bank			
passport application form			
health and safety report on a local company			
novel			
travel brochure			
instructions on how to play a board game			
story in a magazine			

Suggestions for Activity 7

Not as easy as it looked perhaps. Instructions for operating a DVD player would clearly be an *explanatory* text. But you may have been unsure which column to tick for some texts. This is because some of them could fall into more than one category. For example, a travel brochure could be seen as *explanatory* because it gives prices, flight details and locations, but it could also be *persuasive* because of the audience at which it is aimed. The cover would be designed to attract people to a type of holiday and there would be colour and pictures inside to sell holidays.

© National Extension College Trust Ltd

Type of text	Explanatory	Persuasive	Descriptive
DIY manual	✓		
guide to a museum	✓		✓
letter to a local newspaper arguing the case for foxhunting		✓	
instructions for operating a DVD player	✓		
newspaper report of a football match			✓
booklet with details of the services offered by a bank		✓	
passport application form	✓		
health and safety report on a local company			✓
novel			✓
travel brochure	✓	✓	
instructions on how to play a board game	✓		
story in a magazine			✓

Now try this activity in which you will think further about how to categorise texts in this way.

Activity 8

Hint

Don't just read the words. Look at the layout and pictures too.

Read the following texts. They have all been written with a particular audience in mind and a message for that audience.

1   For each text tick a column in the table to say whether you think it is explanatory (E), persuasive (P) or descriptive (D) or a combination of all three (All).

2   For each one think about the audience, message and purpose and say whether or not you think it is effective. Give reasons for your answer.

3   Suggest improvements to the texts.

Text	E	P	D	All	Is it effective?Why/why not?	Ideas for improvement
1						
2						
3						
4						

Text 1

FIRE PRECAUTIONS REGULATIONS 2002

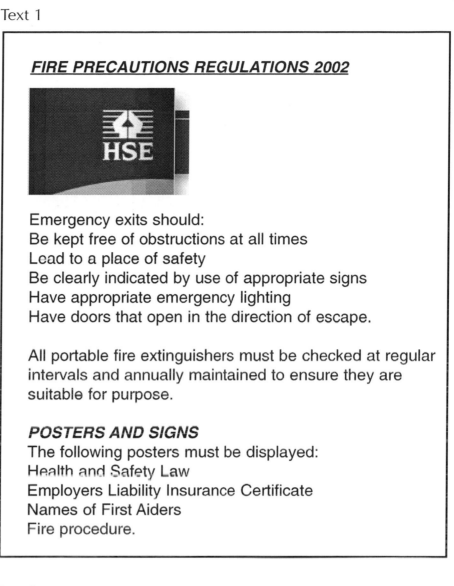

Emergency exits should:
Be kept free of obstructions at all times
Lead to a place of safety
Be clearly indicated by use of appropriate signs
Have appropriate emergency lighting
Have doors that open in the direction of escape.

All portable fire extinguishers must be checked at regular intervals and annually maintained to ensure they are suitable for purpose.

POSTERS AND SIGNS
The following posters must be displayed:
Health and Safety Law
Employers Liability Insurance Certificate
Names of First Aiders
Fire procedure.

Text 2

There are two alarm settings for your selection. You can either set Alarm 1 or Alarm 2 or you can select both Alarms. The alarm tones of 1 and 2 are different from each other. To set Alarm 1 enter the Mode key and press Set. When the hour and minute digits are flashing press the time you want to show. When finished press Set and the alarm automatically switches on to alarm.

Text 3

TRANSPORT CLERK

The Company is a highly successful MDF producer with an annual turnover in excess of £23 million and employing around 800 staff nationwide. A vacancy has arisen in the Transport Department to support the work of our Transport Manager and Transport Supervisor. The successful applicant will have excellent communication skills, be able to use the telephone with confidence and have a working knowledge of computers. Duties will include general office administration, manual and computer routing for transport liaison with hauliers and external customers.

For an application form please contact the Personnel Department on 01234 567891.

Text 4

DISABILITY HOUSING OFFICER
Salary £16,000–£20,000
To work in Northend Park
The main role of the job will be to develop outreach work for both housing and disability advice. You will be required to give aid and advice on legal rights, welfare benefits and housing.

Qualifications Needed: Diploma in Social Work
EXPERIENCE: Four years minimum

START DATE
1 October
Please apply in writing to:
The Director, Social Services, County Hall, Northend

Suggestions for Activity 8

Your ideas should be something like this

Text	E	P	D	All	Is it effective? Why/why not?	Ideas for improvement
1			✓		Yes. Good use of lists. Good use of bold and underlining. Not too much information on the page.	Suggest using bullet points and putting them in double spacing.
2	✓				Not really. Information is difficult to follow. Not very friendly. Too much information in one paragraph will confuse people.	Suggest putting each point on a separate line, perhaps numbering them or using bullet points. Suggest using bold or capitals to highlight important words such as SET.
3				✓	Quite effective. Good idea to use picture and headings but too much information and not well spaced out.	Suggest including missed important information such as salary, hours, holiday entitlement etc.
4				✓	Yes. It uses a picture to catch people's attention and the information is set out clearly so that it can be read easily. All the important information is included. Good use of headings, bold and italics.	Suggest replacing the picture with one that is more relevant to the job.

Reflective learning log

Make notes on three things you have read in the past three weeks and say if they were descriptive, explanatory or persuasive. Did you come across anything you felt came under more than one heading?

Send the notes to your tutor with the second assignment.

You should be getting the hang of this now. The next activity will give you more practice in recognising types of text.

Activity 9

Hint

Be careful when you answer as the message the article is putting across is not as simple as it seems.

Read the following article and then answer the questions below.

SMOKERS ASK TO BE SERVED WITH A BAN

Smokers should be barred from restaurants, a new poll published today says.

Even smokers themselves would be in favour of a ban on this filthy habit says the Department of Health.

The message comes as statistics show that 100,000 people died from smoking-related illnesses last year, all of which could have been avoided.

The survey reveals that at least 56% of households contain one or more smokers who would rather not eat in a restaurant full of customers puffing away. And almost half of them supported a complete ban on smoking in eating areas. This shows the dangers and anti-social nature of smokers who are more than happy to waste their money with no regard for others.

Anne Robinson, a spokesperson for the Department of Health, said yesterday that over 70% of adults in the UK are non-smokers so it is likely that a large majority of customers in restaurants are non-smokers. An increasing number of people now say they would leave a restaurant if tables for non-smokers were not available.

Three million people in this country suffer from asthma and other people smoking are a major contributor to attacks.

This disgusting habit needs to be stamped out completely and if it was we could save billions of pounds on the National Health Service.

1   Do you feel the article is explanatory, persuasive or descriptive? Explain your answer.

2   Do you feel the article is fair? Explain your answer.

Suggestions for Activity 9

1   It is *persuasive* as it is trying to convince people that smoking is a bad habit. It gives figures and refers to a government report to back up its arguments. It also makes important points about the rights of non-smokers in restaurants.

2   I would say that it is not absolutely fair because the opposite point of view (of people who want to smoke in restaurants) isn't given.

Activity 10

Find an article in a newspaper that you feel is persuasive.

1   Make a few notes below saying why you think it is persuasive.

2   Put yourself in the position of someone who disagrees with the person who wrote the article. Using a separate sheet of paper, plan a reply to the article.

Cross-reference

If you want to find out more about writing a letter, try Section 1 in the 'Writing' module.

Reflective learning log

1   Make a note in your learning log of the key features of explanatory, persuasive and descriptive texts.

2   Think about how the way you read has changed since you started this section. Are you stopping to think before you read material? Make notes in your learning log.

Self-check 2

Write in the type of text for the following.

Text	Persuasive/Explanatory/ Descriptive
DIY manual	
Letter to a newspaper on foxhunting	
Short story	
A company newsletter	
Soap powder advertisement	
Television programmes listing	
Set of instructions for a CD player	
Coach timetable	
Tourist Information leaflet	
Cricket scores	

Our suggestions for Self-Check 2 are at the end of the section.

Summary

In Topic 2 you have looked at formal and informal texts, and the differences between explanatory, persuasive and descriptive texts.

By completing Topic 2 you have done more work on point 2 of the 'Text Focus' section of the Adult Literacy Core Curriculum, but have also covered point 4. Grammar and punctuation have also been covered ('Sentence Focus').

Section summary

The activities in this section should have helped you to recognise the types of text you are likely to come across. They will also have given you practice in the scanning, skimming and intensive reading techniques you looked at in Section 1.

Reflective learning log

Make a note of some of the things you have learned from the two topics in Section 2. Write down anything about your reading that you think has improved as a result of working through this section. As you work through the rest of the Reading module make a note in your learning log if you use the things you have learned in this section.

Suggestions for Self-check 2

Here are my suggestions.

Text	Persuasive/Explanatory/Descriptive
DIY manual	Explanatory
Letter to a newspaper on foxhunting	Persuasive
Short story	Descriptive
A company newsletter	Descriptive
Soap powder advertisement	Persuasive
Television programmes listing	Explanatory
Set of instructions for a CD player	Explanatory
Coach timetable	Explanatory
Tourist Information leaflet	Persuasive
Cricket scores	Descriptive

If you are not sure, check through this section again.

Section 3: Identifying the main points of a text

Section 3: Identifying the main points of a text

In this section you will be looking at how you can pick out the main points of a text. This will help you take information from texts quickly and efficiently.

Topic 1: Highlighting information

This topic is about highlighting information. This means picking out the most important information in a text and making it stand out from what is not so important. Highlighting information while you read is a useful skill because it helps you to identify the key points of a text. You can then return to a text at a later date (e.g. when revising for an exam) and you won't need to read the whole text again.

When you are highlighting you only need to highlight key words or phrases. You can do this by underlining words, or using a highlighter pen. If you are a person who learns more by looking at things rather than listening, you might like to use two or more highlighting colours to help you remember the key points.

Reasons for completing this topic

This topic will help you to:

● identify the purposes of a text

● select the most important parts of text.

Try this first activity, which asks you to highlight the main points of a newspaper article.

Activity 1

Read the following newspaper report and highlight what you think are the three main points.

BENEFIT FRAUDSTER IS FINED

Walkland District Council has issued a warning after a mail order clerk was fined for fraudulently obtaining benefits.

Thomas Wilkinson, aged 64 of South London, admitted three charges at the Magistrates Court of fraudulently obtaining benefits amounting to £7,500.

He admitted failing to disclose income from distributing mail order goods during part-time employment.

Wilkinson was sentenced to 200 hours Community Service and is currently repaying the money.

John Stevens of the Walkland District Council Finance Office said 'genuine' claimants have nothing to fear, but the Council takes a very serious view of housing benefit fraud. Any changes in circumstances should be referred to the District Council immediately.

Suggestions for Activity 1

Check your answers with our suggestions below.

Looking at the title, I think the article is mainly about benefit fraud. So I would highlight these three points:

    fraudulently obtaining benefits

    sentenced to 200 hours community service

    failing to disclose income.

Now try the next two activities to check your highlighting skills.

Activity 2

Hint

Remember that you are looking for clues from the text as to what the author feels is important.

Buy a quality (broadsheet) newspaper such as *The Times*, *Guardian* or *The Independent*.

1   Find an article that contains at least five paragraphs. Read through the article quickly and highlight the five main points of the article, underlining or with a highlighter pen.

2   Summarise the article below in about 15 words.

3   Write your own headline for the article.

4   Make a note below saying what made this exercise easy or difficult, e.g. headlines, paragraphs.

Suggestions for Activity 2

Highlighting is a skill that does improve quickly with practice. Your answers will obviously depend on the article you chose.

As a general rule, for a newspaper article, you should start by looking at the headline because that should summarise what the article is about. The first and last paragraphs might also sum up the whole article. In a newspaper there are also sometimes photographs with captions that give clues.

Now try your highlighting skills again with the next two passages.

Activity 3

1   Read the following text in no more than 15 seconds (use a watch or timer to time yourself). Highlight what you feel to be the most important points. Cover it with a sheet of paper and answer the questions that follow.

Lunchtime Supervisor – Team Leader

£6.25 per hour

This is an important new role as a co-ordinator and supervisor of the School's team of lunchtime supervisors.

Applicants should be enthusiastic, flexible and committed to ensuring that the aims of the school are implemented in all areas of our lunchtime activities

For application forms and further details contact **Michael White** at the school.

Closing date is two weeks from the date of the advert.

---

a)   What is the job?

b)   What are the duties of the post?

c)   Who should applicants contact?

d)   When is the closing date?

e)   What is the rate of pay per hour?

Uncover the text and check your answers.

2   Read the following text in no more than 15 seconds (use a watch or timer to time yourself). Highlight the most important points. Cover it with a sheet of paper and answer the questions that follow.

Outdoor activities in the Dales area range from mountain biking to horse riding. In North Yorkshire the hostels have a full complement of trained instructors. Scarborough is the cheapest of our coastal centres so it is popular with the younger age group. The scenery in the area is second to none and there is a wide range of excursions available from here and both the other coastal centres we have in the north. There are no organised excursions in other areas. For those of you who like peace and quiet Devon is recommended. Our properties are located just over the border from Cornwall and this reflects the nature of the holiday experience there. Again there is a range of activities but no organised excursions. We obviously cannot guarantee the weather in our centres so it is advisable that you bring full waterproofs with you and have a change of clothing for each day you will be on site. Payment of the full costs of the holiday will need to be made one month in advance; these are non-refundable.

a)   Where is the hostel in North Yorkshire situated?

b)   From where are excursions available?

c)   Which area is recommended if you like peace and quiet?

d)   Is payment refundable?

e)   When do you pay the full costs of the holiday?

Uncover the text and check your answers.

3   Did you find it easier to extract information from one of the texts? If so, which one? Write down why you think this was so.

Suggestions for Activity 3

I found the second text more difficult to read than the first. There was too much writing and not enough clues as to where you had to stop or which were the important points in the passage.

The first text had a lot of clues as to the message the author wanted to get over:

    a)   bold type

    b)   headings in the middle

    c)   short paragraphs.

This made it easier to extract the information.

Reflective learning log

Write down some notes on how the speed of your reading has changed and what things in a text are helping you to find the most important points.

Summary

In Topic 1 you have looked at the very important skill of selecting the main points from a text. This is an important starting point for becoming an efficient reader. Once you have that skill, the speed and efficiency of your reading will improve quickly.

> By completing Topic 1 you have covered point 3 of the 'Text Focus' section of the Adult Literacy Core Curriculum: 'identify the main points and specific details'. You will also have practised grammar and punctuation ('Sentence Focus').

    © National Extension College Trust Ltd

Topic 2: Reading longer documents

The highlighting skills you practised in Topic 1 may be especially important when you are reading longer documents. With a longer document, you will need to be able to identify many more key points at the same time as keeping in your mind the overall message of the document. We will look at this in detail in this topic. In Topic 3 we will focus on one kind of longer document – a report. In Section 6 we will look at reading technical documents.

Reasons for completing this topic

This topic will help you to:

- summarise information from longer documents
- practise skimming, scanning and reading in depth.

What kinds of longer documents might you want to read?

Start by thinking about the different kinds of longer documents you might want to read.

Activity 4

> List as many longer documents as you can under the three headings below.
>
> a) You personally   b) You may have to   c) You are not likely
>   have had to read   read in future   to have to read
>
>
>
>
>
>
>
>
>
>
>
>
>
>
> Continue on a separate sheet of paper if you need to.

Suggestions for Activity 4

There are no 'correct' answers to this activity. What you have written will depend on your experience and expectations. Here are my ideas:

a) have to	b) might have to	c) probably never read
local planning permission proposals	College Governors Reports	technical manuals
College Inspection Report	computer manuals	video instructions
report on new cars	History textbooks	medical books
report on effectiveness of new teaching material	car repair manual	Scottish Nuclear Power Report
newspaper articles on educational subjects	guidebook for a city	cookery book

What can you do to improve your reading of longer documents?

Go back and quickly read through the main points of Topic 2 in Section 1.

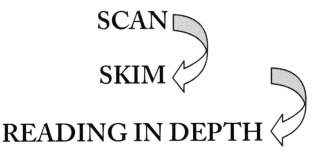

SCAN

SKIM

READING IN DEPTH

Remembering the following letters will help you:

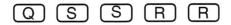

Q   S   S   R   R

These stand for:

QUESTION

Ask yourself:

●   What do I already know about the subject?

●   What do I want from the text?

SKIM AND SCAN

- Look at the titles, headings and sub-headings.

- Look at the captions under pictures, charts, graphs or maps.

- Read introductory and concluding paragraphs.

Ask yourself is this material what I need?

READ

Look for the answers you first raised.

REVIEW

- Ask yourself questions about what you have just read.

- Ask yourself questions at the end about what you have just read.

- Read any notes you may have taken.

Activity 5

Hint
The article is about children's attitude to food.

Using the method described above, read the following article (adapted from an article in *Guardian*, July 1999).

THE FIGHT OVER FOOD

Over 50% of children under the age of five will at some stage have had problems with eating and over 20% of families admit that their younger children have caused severe domestic problems by their refusal to eat certain foods and in some extreme cases refusing to eat at all.

A study published recently by the Co-op found that over two-thirds of children had gone through a phase of refusing to eat a particular food and almost one in twenty will refuse anything that is put in front of them.

Children were found to dislike a wide range of foods but the most disliked were sprouts disliked by 40%, cabbage disliked by 30%, tomatoes 28%, turnips and onions 15% and beetroot with 10%.

Children react to various foods for a range of reasons. Obviously the list of foods that proved the most unpopular did not contain any sweet foods and on the whole it was the foods that parents saw as the healthiest which were ignored.

Activity 5 continued

This difference of opinion could be the real explanation of the refusal of children to eat certain foods. It is obvious from the study that younger children see food as a way of rebelling against parental control and the way in which parents handle early refusals is important to what the child's behaviour will be like in later years. If parents make a fuss over a child's refusal to eat certain foods the child will mainly react by refusing more foods. The message to parents seems to be that if your child refuses to eat let them get on with it! There is no evidence of a child suffering medical problems due to a self-imposed diet.

The reasons for the child's behaviour need to be examined. One child refused to eat bacon after learning that it came from pigs, animals with which he had just become acquainted with after a visit to a local Farm Park. The impact of advertising can also be put forward as an explanation for a child's behaviour. Children are constantly bombarded by advertisements for what most adults would classify as unhealthy foods.

Parents often complain that they are blackmailed by TV adverts which promote junk food and drink. Advertisers are accused of using cynical blackmail tactics to target children and exploit their vulnerability; a recent report suggests that despite

evidence that British children are increasingly unhealthy they are constantly being fed a continuous diet of television commercials promoting fatty, sugary and salty products. A recent survey showed that 99% of food adverts broadcast during children's television programmes on Saturday mornings advertised food which contained either high fat, sugar or salt.

In conclusion we can say that the problem of children refusing to eat is not as serious as a lot of people seem to think. Children who watch a lot of television can use pester power against their parents but the studies done to date tend to suggest that no lasting harm will come to children and fads go as children grow up.

Hint

You may not get all the answers right. This is a long and complicated passage, so don't worry. We are aiming here for practice, rather than being totally correct.

1   Cover the text with a sheet of paper and try to answer the questions below.

   a)   What percentage of children do not like cabbage?

   b)   What percentage of children do not like tomatoes?

   c)   Who published the recent study on eating habits?

d)   What reasons does the article suggest for children having food fads?

e)   What does the article include as unhealthy foods?

f)   Does the article consider food fads in children to be serious? How do you know?

2   Uncover the article and fill any gaps in your answers.

3   Cover the article again with a sheet of paper. Write down below what you feel were the four main points of the article.

a)

b)

c)

d)

4   Re-read the article and write down below what you now feel the main points are.

Make a note of any differences between this answer and your answer to 2.

a)

b)

c)

d)

Suggestions for Activity 5

Don't worry if your answers aren't exactly the same as mine. Just think of how you came to find the main points and how you could apply the same methods to other longer documents you may read.

1 and 2

    a)   30%

    b)   28%

    c)   The Co-op

    d)   Children see food as a way of rebelling against parental control.

    e)   Those containing either high fat, sugar or salt.

    f)   No. It says, 'We can say that the problem of children refusing to eat is not as serious as a lot of people seem to think'.

3   a)   Some children refuse food.

    b)   Parents have problems when children refuse food.

    c)   Advertisers should be criticised for promoting unhealthy foods to children.

    d)   The problem is probably not as serious as parents think.

4   Your answers will be individual to you.

How difficult did you find each stage of this activity? I would be surprised if you had managed to get all the answers to part 1 right. The article is fairly complicated and did not have many signposts to help you highlight the key points. Also, you were reading without a purpose in that you did not know what questions were going to be asked.

You will have done better on part 2 because you knew what questions you needed to answer.

Part 3 should have been even easier as you had read the passage a number of times by then and were aware of what was in it. Note any differences between the stages and ask yourself why this happened.

Reflective learning log

Make a note of your thoughts about summarising in your learning log. Think of any long texts you have read recently. If you were asked to read them again would you be able to summarise them?

Summary

In Topic 2 you have looked at reading longer documents. To someone who is just beginning to think about reading such material this may seem frightening, but hopefully you will have seen that it is not as difficult as it first looks. Remember to practise the skills you are now learning at every opportunity.

By completing Topic 2 you have covered point 8 of the 'Text Focus' section of the Adult Literacy Core Curriculum: 'summarise information from longer documents'.

Topic 3:　Reading reports

In this topic you will be looking at reading reports. Examples of reports include:

- newspaper reports, for example, on an accident or a soccer match
- reports written by an employee for their boss
- government reports
- traffic accident reports written by a police officer
- reports of damage written for an insurance company.

There are four main reasons for writing a report:

1　To record information (e.g. a report that provides a record of a road accident).

2　To influence people who are making decisions (e.g. an investigation into building a large estate of houses in a rural area).

3　To start action (e.g. to suggest that a stretch of road should have speed cameras installed).

4　To persuade people (e.g. a government report persuading people to switch to lead-free petrol).

As reports are aimed at different audiences they vary in length, style and layout. We will be looking at this in this topic.

Reasons for completing this topic

This topic will help you to:

- recognise and read different types of report
- practise identifying the main points
- practise different reading techniques.

Which reports have you read?

Start by thinking about the different kinds of reports you have read.

Activity 6

1   Make a list of some of the reports you have read over the past few years in the space below. Re-read the examples above if you can't think of any.

2   Answer these questions.

   a)   Which report do you remember most clearly?

   b   Why do you think the report you remember has stayed in your memory?

Suggestions for Activity 6

The reports I remember are those most relevant to what I needed, such as a report on teachers' pay! They are usually well laid out and signposted so that it is easy to find and remember the key points.

Reflective learning log

Think about what made you remember that report more than the others. Make notes in your learning log.

Formal reports

These are reports written by people who do not know their audience so the language will be more complicated. A good formal report usually contains a number of signposts, such as:

● headings

● sub-headings

● bullet points.

Formal reports are divided into sections, with signposts to what is contained within each section.

Formal reports usually have:

● a contents page

● **terms of reference**

● introduction

● **methodology**

● findings

● conclusion

● recommendations

● **appendices.**

We will look at each of these next.

Cross-reference

If you have already tackled the 'Writing' module, you may want to skip this next part.

Contents page

This is a quick list of the topics covered with page numbers, sometimes with a short summary of each topic.

Terms of reference

These explain why the report was written, the background to the report and the audience it is aimed at.

Introduction

This gives a short explanation of what the report is about. Reading this section is useful if all you need is a quick overview of the report. You can read the introduction together with the conclusion if time is really short and you do not need to challenge or build on the findings of the report.

Methodology

This is a very important part of more academic reports, where the writer explains how they came about their findings – what methods they used. If you are reading a report that you disagree with it is important to read this section. Without this information you would find it difficult to put forward opposite arguments.

Findings

In this section the writer presents their findings and arguments. Findings may also include recommendations, but normally these would appear after the conclusion (see below).

The findings should have a number of signposts to direct you to what the author feels is important. These should include headings, underlining, capitals, and italics or bold letters.

The headings are like chapter headings in a book so you can scan these before you start to read the full report. Headings normally have sub-headings that give a further guide to the findings.

Conclusion

This is a brief summary of the main points and any conclusions the writer has come to.

Recommendations

These are the suggestions for action that arise from the findings of the report. If you have asked for the report to be written, or have a direct interest in the matter, this section needs to be read carefully as it will form the basis for future actions. Recommendations should be written in a way that is easy to read, with bullet points and other signposts.

Appendices

This is where additional information relating to the report is placed. For example, graphs, charts and tables of figures may be placed here rather than in the main body of the report.

In more academic reports, references to other sources are listed in a **bibliography**. Reading a bibliography is not necessary unless you are thinking of researching the topic yourself and writing your own report.

How to read a report

Keep the following guidelines in mind when you next read a long or complicated report:

- question – think carefully about the questions you want the report to answer

- scan or skim – see Section 1 to remind yourself of these skills

- read – see Section 1 to remind yourself of how to read in depth.

Steps to reading reports

1 Read the title: ask yourself 'Is this the right report for me to read?'

2 Read the contents page: 'Does the report contain what I need?'

3 Read the introduction: 'Does the report contain what I need?'

4 Read the conclusion: 'Does the report contain what I need?'

5 Skim through the headings: use a highlighter pen to pick out the main points.

6 Look for signposts to what the author thinks is important – italics, bold, capital letters.

7 Read the important sections.

8 Review what you have read: 'Have I got what I need? If not, what should I read again?'

Activity 7

Read the following report.

You asked me to write a report on the accident in the wood store that occurred yesterday afternoon.

Jon was driving the forklift truck and appears to have lost control when it skidded. I have a feeling that it was due to a patch of oil on the floor, which had been left by one of our fleet lorries. I seem to remember that Jon also has a history of epilepsy so it is possible he had a convulsion and lost control.

In the event he was quite badly hurt so I had to call an ambulance and he was taken to hospital. He seems to have broken his arm and will be off work for the next five weeks.

I would suggest we look at the steering on the forklift truck, as this is the third accident this week. Also, employees need to be warned that if it turns out they are medically unfit to be driving they will not be entitled to compensation and could be dismissed.

Make a note below of what the report contains under each of the headings.

1   Terms of reference

2   Findings

3   Conclusions

4   Recommendations

Suggestions for Activity 7

How did you do? You should have picked out the key features shown below. If you didn't, have another look at the report after reading these answers.

1   Terms of reference – you asked me to write

2   Findings – accident caused by a patch of oil on the floor

3   Conclusions – due to steering of the forklift truck

4   Recommendations – check forklift truck and warn employees.

The next activity is based on a report commissioned by Northamptonshire County Council into crime in Southland, an area of Northampton. It is longer than any of the material you have been reading up to now – so it will be more challenging.

This is a real chance to practise the skills we have talked about so far – so take your time and enjoy it!

Activity 8

Read the following report. The order of the paragraphs has been deliberately mixed up.

REPORT ON CRIME IN SOUTHLAND

In addition to recorded crime Southland Police have also kept records of other incidents reported to them. These are not actual crimes in the sense the perpetrators have committed a criminal offence, but they have given rise to complaints from local residents. These can be divided into juvenile nuisances and breach of the peace. Local vandalism is included in this as are breaches of the peace such as drunkenness and obstruction. The most frequently recorded crimes in the area were burglary and crime against motor vehicles. A comparison of recorded crime in the following year paints a similar picture. There was a slight improvement over the previous year but the percentages remains higher than both the county and the national average.

The most common crimes nationally are assault and offences against cars. National assault rates include grievous bodily harm, actual body harm and a range of offences against the person. Burglary is the third most common crime nationally with aggravated burglary being the least common offence.

Activity 8 continued

The Town Council had expressed concern that there seems to be a growing problem with crime and general disorder in the town and they asked for recommendations as to how the situation could be improved. They requested this account of crime in Southland.

The information that follows is based on a survey of three wards in the town over the past two years. The survey was carried out by a local market research company and cost £30,000.

Residents suggested that juvenile nuisance and breach of the peace were the biggest causes for concern. There was a widespread feeling that facilities for young people were totally inadequate and the main complaints were about teenagers 'hanging around', noisy neighbours and gangs, bad street lighting and young people drinking in public places.

The total number of recorded crimes in Southland in 1998 was 14,777. This represents a crime rate of about 123 per 1,000 residents; that is considerably higher than the rates for both Southland and Northamptonshire as a whole. It is also a quarter higher than for England and Wales as a whole.

The Report would make the following recommendations: an increased police presence in the town centre, the introduction of CCTV cameras in the town centre, the provision of better facilities for younger people, and an increase in car park security systems.

The figures show that during the two years in question there were a total of 4,500 known offenders in Southland. A breakdown of the information illustrates that 77% of these were by males, most offences were committed by offenders aged between 13 and 27, 67% of all motor vehicle crime was committed by offenders under the age of 16, the most common offence committed by offenders aged 18 to 20 was burglary.

The majority of all age groups felt safe in the Town Centre but this fell at night, as shown in the table. This appears to be in line with the experiences of towns and cities on a national scale, where the character of the town centre is often different to that of the rest of the town.

Activity 8 continued

1   When you have read the report, decide on the correct order for the paragraphs and number the paragraphs starting with 1 for the first paragraph. Why do you think the order you have chosen is right? Jot down your notes in the space below.

2   When you have put the paragraphs in what you feel is the correct order, write down in the table below where you think the following headings should appear. We have done the first one for you.

Feature	Where the heading should appear
Terms of reference	before paragraph 3
Introduction	
Methodology	
Findings	
Conclusions	
Recommendations	

3   Some of the paragraphs contain information that could probably be presented more effectively by using a list of bullet points. Choose two paragraphs that you think could be better presented in this way and rewrite them on a separate sheet of paper.

4   Write down below where you would put the charts. Explain your reasons.

Suggestions for Activity 8

Here is our rewritten version of the passage. Have a look and see if it matches your answers. Don't worry if it isn't exactly the same as there is no correct answer, but think about why I have written my version in this way. Think in particular where I have put my headings and sub-headings.

REPORT ON CRIME IN SOUTHLAND

Terms of reference

The Town Council had expressed concern that there seems to be a growing problem with crime and general disorder in the town and they asked for recommendations as to how the situation could be improved. They requested this account of crime in Southland.

Methodology

The information that follows is based on a survey of three wards in the town over the past two years. The survey was carried out by a local market research company and cost £30,000.

Findings

- <u>Number of crimes</u>

  The total number of recorded crimes in Southland in 1998 was 14,777. This represents a crime rate of about 123 per 1,000 residents; that is considerably higher than the rates for both Southland and Northamptonshire as a whole. It is also a quarter higher than for England and Wales as a whole.

- <u>Type of crime</u>

  The most frequently recorded crimes in the area were burglary and crime against motor vehicles. A comparison of recorded crime in the following year paints a similar picture. There was a slight improvement over the previous year but the percentages remains higher than both the county and the national average.

- <u>The national picture</u>

  The most common crimes nationally are assault and offences against cars. National assault rates include grievous bodily harm, actual body harm and a range of offences against the person. Burglary is the third most common crime nationally with aggravated burglary being the least common offence.

- ● <u>Types of offenders</u>

  The figures show that during the two years in question there were a total of 4,500 known offenders in Southland. A breakdown of the information illustrates that:

  - ● 77% of these were male, most offences were committed by offenders aged between 13 and 27

  - ● 67% of all motor vehicle crime was committed by offenders under the age of 16

  - ● the most common offence committed by offenders aged 18 to 20 was burglary.

- ● <u>Other types of crime</u>

  In addition to recorded crime, Southland Police have also kept records of other incidents reported to them. These are not actual crimes in the sense the perpetrators have committed a criminal offence, but they have given rise to complaints from local residents. These can be divided into juvenile nuisances and breach of the peace. Local vandalism is included in this, as are breaches of the peace such as drunkenness and obstruction.

  Residents suggested that juvenile nuisance and breach of the peace were the biggest causes for concern. There was a widespread feeling that facilities for young people were totally inadequate and the main complaints were about teenagers 'hanging around', noisy neighbours and gangs, bad street lighting and young people drinking in public places.

- ● <u>The town centre</u>

  The majority of all age groups felt safe in the town centre but this fell at night, as shown in the table. This appears to be in line with the experiences of towns and cities on a national scale, where the character of the town centre is often different to that of the rest of the town.

Recommendations

The Report would make the following recommendations:

- ● an increased police presence in the town centre

- ● the introduction of CCTV cameras in the town centre

- ● the provision of better facilities for younger people

- ● an increase in car park security systems.

Reflective learning log

1. Do you think this activity will help with writing reports as well as reading them? If so, make a note in your learning log of why you think this.

2. Make a note of some of the things you have learned from the two topics in Section 1. Write down anything about your reading that you think has improved as a result of working through this section. As you work through the rest of the module try to make a note in your learning log if you use the things you have learned in this section.

Summary

In Topic 3 you have looked at reading reports and practised different reading techniques.

Now try this self-check exercise.

Self-check 3

1   Write down:
    a)   the useful signposts in a text

    b)   the sections of a formal report

    c)   what the letters Q S S R R mean.

Self-check 3 continued

2   Read the following passage taken from a Department of Health leaflet.

a)   Give the passage a title.

b)   Reduce the passage to 50 words.

c)   Then reduce it to about 15 words.

The legal limit for driving is 80 mg of alcohol in every 100ml of blood. In practice, there are many factors which can affect an individual's ability to stay under this legal limit and so there is no fail-safe guide as to how much a person can drink before being illegal to drive.

About 90% of the adult population in Britain drinks to some extent. The average amount for men is the equivalent of eight pints of beer per week and for women the equivalent of three pints per week.

Alcohol is absorbed into the bloodstream and has an effect within five or ten minutes. The effect can last for several hours, depending on the amount consumed.

Suggestions for Self-check 3 are given on the next page.

Section summary

You should now be able to read long documents more quickly and more efficiently. You have practised highlighting and summarising, and reading longer documents, including reports. Hopefully you will now be seeing how highlighting and summarising are fitting together with scanning, skimming and reading in depth.

> By completing Topic 3 you have covered point 8 of the 'Text Focus' section of the Adult Literacy Core Curriculum: 'summarise information from longer documents'.

Hint

Your version may be different to mine, but don't worry. You should have recognised the main points which appeared in my 50-word version.

Suggestions for Self-check 3

Here are my suggestions:

1 a) headings

        sub-headings

        bullet points.

   b) Formal reports usually have:

        ● a contents page

        ● terms of reference

        ● introduction

        ● methodology

        ● findings

        ● conclusion

        ● recommendations

        ● appendices.

   c) Question; Skim and Scan; Read; Review.

2 a) Drinking and Driving

   b) The legal limit for driving is 80 mg in every 100 ml. It is not possible to say how much a person can drink before driving legally. About 90% of people in Britain drink: men eight pints on average; women three. Alcohol has an effect within five or ten minutes.

   c) Impossible to advise on legal limit for drinking and driving.

Section 4: Reading and understanding arguments

Section 4: Reading and understanding arguments

Welcome to Section 4 of the Reading module. The next step to being a good reader is to be able to recognise arguments in texts. We have already considered this briefly in Section 2 when we looked at persuasive texts. In this section we will be looking in more detail at how we can recognise arguments in texts, so that we can judge whether a text is biased or prejudiced, and whether it is based on fact or opinion. The activities will also help you to see how punctuation and grammar can affect the meaning of texts.

Topic 1: Recognising the arguments in a text

This first topic is about recognising arguments in texts. This allows us to understand the difference between fact and opinion.

Reasons for completing this topic

This topic will enable you to think about:

● how a writer's point of view can affect the way they write a text

● how important it is to be able to tell the difference between what is true and what is the opinion of the writer.

Let's start with an activity designed to check on your learning from Section 2.

Activity 1

Look up the words 'prejudice' and 'bias' in a dictionary. Write down below a sentence for each showing how it could be used. For example:

'He is definitely prejudiced against women – he never promotes them at work.'

Prejudice

Bias

Check your responses with our suggestions below, before continuing.

Suggestions for Activity 1

Here are our definitions. The definition in your dictionary may be slightly different but should have the same general meaning.

Prejudice – an opinion against a group or individual based on insufficient facts and usually unfavourable and/or intolerant.

Sentence: He was prejudiced against foreign people and wanted to stop all immigration into this country.

Bias – very similar to but not as extreme as prejudice. Someone who is biased usually refuses to accept that there are other views than their own.

Sentence: All the football reports in the local newspaper were biased against visiting teams because the Editor is a Melchester Rovers supporter.

The next activity will help you to recognise bias and prejudice.

Activity 2

Read the following letters. They have been adapted from letters to a national newspaper.

Letter 1

Dear Sir

The decision to build a new terminal at Stansted Airport is a clear indication that this Government has finally abandoned any pretence of listening to local opinion and are determined to discredit and dismantle any of the remaining rights that local people have to a say in the future of their environment.

No sensible argument has been put forward for the extension. The real losers in this argument are local people. It seems that if you choose to live by an airport you then give up the right to have a say in local matters.

The private sector is the only opinion the Government seems to want to listen to. The wishes of local people are now totally ignored in the planning process.

We all want to see a decent, well-planned travel system but this is not the way to go about it. Everybody should be involved, not just big business.

Yours faithfully

Letter 2

Dear Sir

The announcement that the Stansted extension will go ahead will mean a noise pollution and traffic nightmare for tens of thousands of people living near and around the airport. It must be stopped before it is too late.

The new terminal will bring a horrendous increase in traffic, it is estimated that there will be an increase of over 30 million passengers every year. This is totally unacceptable and we must fight to the death to oppose it. It is simply dreadful that the people of North Essex be made to suffer for the greed of the rest of the country.

It is disgraceful and totally unnecessary that noise and air pollution should be allowed to grow to what will be a deadly level.

Yours faithfully

**Activity 2
continued**

Answer the questions below.

1   Is the writer of Letter 1 for or against the extension to the airport? How do you know?

2   What would you say are the main arguments the writer uses in Letter 1 to support their point of view?

3   Is the writer of Letter 2 for or against the extension to the airport? How do you know?

4   Write down below the type of words both writers use to try to get their point of view across.

     Letter 1

     Letter 2

5   Which letter do you think is the most biased? Explain your reasons.

Suggestions for Activity 2

Here are some ideas. You should have spotted that Letter 2 is more biased, uses more **sensational words** and more emotive language than Letter 1.

1 It is difficult to say if the writer of Letter 1 is for or against the extension to the airport. The letter is really about the way in which the decision was taken, without consulting local people.

2 The writer is saying that the planning process has been ignored and that local people should have been involved in the decision.

3 The writer of Letter 2 is obviously against the extension.

4 The words used in Letter 1 are not as strong as in Letter 2. The language used in Letter 2 is sensational and emotional and is aimed at convincing people that the extension is a bad thing.

5 Letter 2 is more biased because the writer obviously feels there is only one view: that the extension is a bad thing.

If you can quickly recognise a writer's point of view or see language that is unfair, you can make better decisions about the value of the text. As an active reader you need to keep the writer's position in mind and always be ready to think of other arguments that might give balance.

Reflective learning log

Write down a list of issues that you think could arouse strong emotions in people and perhaps cause them to write unbalanced or unfair material.

Fact and opinion

It is very important, as an active reader, to recognise the difference between **fact** and **opinion** in texts. Facts will be true and cannot be argued with, while opinions will vary with the attitudes of the writer. It is important to remember, however, that facts can often be twisted to fit the opinions of the writer.

Now try Activity 3, which looks at the differences between fact and opinion.

Activity 3

Without using a dictionary, write down below what you think is meant by the following words.

Fact

Opinion

Suggestions for Activity 3

Here are our ideas. Yours might not be exactly the same but should be similar.

Fact – Something that is true and can be proved.

Opinion – A person's view. It may or may not be backed up by facts.

The link between fact and opinion

When people are writing articles and reports they often select facts that support their opinion. When you are reading these kinds of documents you need to be able to tell the difference between facts that can be backed up by evidence and facts that have been made up by the writer. You can do this by:

● checking that any facts or reports quoted actually exist

● trying to find or think of other material or sources that give opposing points of view

● thinking of the audience for whom the text has been written (for example, articles in a popular newspaper may have been written to sell newspapers rather than to give a true or fair account of an incident)

● looking for sensational words, such as 'horror' or 'disgraceful', which might *influence* readers' opinions.

Reflective learning log

Make a list of as many sensational words as you can think of. Write down any texts where you have seen those words used.

Now try Activity 4, which looks at the differences between fact and opinion in newspaper reports.

Activity 4

Read the following two extracts from newspaper reports of the same accident.

Article 1

5 SURVIVE HORROR CAR PLUNGE OFF BEACHY HEAD

Five teenagers had a miraculous escape when their car plunged 150 feet off a cliff.

Horrified witnesses were convinced that the three boys and two girls were dead after their car shot backwards over Beachy Head.

Incredibly the pals all survived the death crash but two of the teenagers are critically ill in hospital.

The driver aged 17 had just passed his test. There is no suspicion that any of the teenagers had been taking drugs before the crash although the driver was too ill to take a breathalyser test.

Article 2

FIVE IN CAR SURVIVE FALL OFF BEACHY HEAD CLIFF

Five teenagers fell more than 150 feet in their car when they crashed off a cliff near Beachy Head yesterday. Their Ford Fiesta landed on its bonnet on boulders at the bottom of the cliff. The three boys and two girls were taken by helicopter to Eastbourne General Hospital and two girls and one boy were in a critical condition last night. The police said the teenagers had had a remarkable escape and they did not face prosecution.

1   Which article would you say was the most accurate – 1 or 2?

2   Which contains more facts and which contains more opinions?

Most facts

Most opinions

Suggestions for Activity 4

1   Article 2 is more accurate.

2   Article 2 has more facts. Article 1 has more opinions.

Article 1 is more sensational than Article 2 and probably appeared in a popular newspaper. The clues that Article 1 is based on opinion rather than fact include the following:

● it uses emotional language such as 'horror', 'miraculous', 'incredibly'

● it is also unfair as it mentions drugs and alcohol although there was no direct evidence of either

● it contains bias and prejudice.

It is interesting how the use of words has changed what was a tragic accident into an opinion on teenage drivers, drugs and alcohol.

Article 2 is fairer and simply gives the facts of the crash. It does not try to place the blame on anyone or *sensationalise* the events.

Now try Activity 5, which gives you more practice in recognising the difference between facts and opinions.

Activity 5

Read the following extract, which is adapted from an article in a national newspaper. Using two highlighter pens, highlight facts in one colour and opinions in another colour.

A GRAVE WARNING ON CIGARETTES

Smokers today were warned that lighting up just one cigarette knocks 11 minutes off their life span.

Using statistics for the average male smoker, it has been calculated that regular smoking cuts six and a half years off a person's life. This is based on a man smoking an average of 16 cigarettes a day from the age of 17 until he dies at 71. Over a lifetime the average male smoker consumes 311,003 cigarettes.

Smoking a pack of 20 brings us 3 hours 40 minutes nearer to death – the time it takes to watch the movie *Titanic*, or to run the London Marathon.

Smoking a carton of 200 knocks a day and a half off your life.

The warning about smoking comes as a predicted 1.3 million people try to kick the habit.

Dr Shaw, a Research Fellow at the School of Geographical Science, said that the first day of the New Year was traditionally a time when smokers tried to stop. She admitted that although the calculations about the effect of smoking on length of life published in the *British Medical Journal* today were crude it was a simple way of illustrating the perils of smoking.

Clive Bates, the director of anti-smoking pressure group Action on Smoking and Health (ASH) said, 'This is just another illustration of why smoking is a disgusting habit'.

Suggestions for Activity 5

These are facts, as I saw them on first reading:

● lighting up just one cigarette knocks 11 minutes off a life span

● over a lifetime the average male smoker consumes 311,003 cigarettes

● smoking a packet of 200 cigarettes knocks a day and a half off your life.

This is the opinion of the director of ASH:

'This is just another illustration of why smoking is a disgusting habit.'

This is a good example of where we can be misled by what appears to be the truth. On first reading, I thought all the statistics about smoking affecting the length of life were facts and took the article to be a fair description of the impact of smoking on health. On second reading, however, it seems that the figures themselves cannot be trusted. According to the doctor, they are 'crude' – which could mean inaccurate.

Activity 6

Hint
Remember to look for the signposts – layout, language, pictures.

Select a story that has been reported in both the newspapers you have collected for this section and read the articles carefully.

1   Write down below the main things you notice about the way the story has been reported. What are the main differences?

Main features of the way the story has been reported

Article 1

Article 2

Main differences

Activity 6 continued

2   Read the whole of both newspapers. Can you see any:

●   bias?

●   prejudice?

●   emotional language?

Make notes below.

Broadsheet

Tabloid

Hint

Look at the advertisements in your newspapers. These will give you clues as to the intended audience.

3   What do you think would be the backgrounds of most of the people who read these newspapers? Give reasons for your answer.

Broadsheet

Tabloid

Suggestions for Activity 6

1 and 2   It is difficult to make suggestions without reading the
newspapers, but I would have looked for:

- sensational language, particularly in the headlines

- sensational pictures

- bias in the **editorials** of the newspapers.

Remember the journalists are writing for the people who buy
the newspapers so stories are slanted towards keeping them
interested.

3   We can get clues about who reads a newspaper by looking at the
advertisements. Advertisers will only buy space in a newspaper if it is
going to be seen by the type of people who buy their products. The
broadsheets, for example, are aimed at those who earn more money
and so will contain adverts for foreign holidays or more expensive
cars. The types of words used can also give clues: the tabloids will
use shorter words and shorter articles than the broadsheets.

Reflective learning log

Write down two lists – one for the tabloids, one for the broadsheets. Write
down some notes on the differences between them.

Summary

In this section you have started to think about how a writer's point of
view can affect the way they write a text. You have also seen how
important it is to be able to tell the difference between what is true and
what is the opinion of the writer.

Doing this makes us *critical* readers – a crucial step in becoming *good*
readers.

> By completing Section 4 you have covered point 4 of the 'Text
> Focus' section of the Adult Literacy core curriculum: 'read an
> argument and identify the points of view'. You have also covered
> some grammar and punctuation ('Sentence Focus').

Self-check 4

Read the following two extracts from a letter to a national daily newspaper.

Extract 1

It is interesting how often those in favour of fox hunting will justify this form of animal abuse by explaining that it is essential that foxes are killed and this is less cruel than shooting them.

I am bemused by this often repeated argument as so many of those who oppose shooting foxes are the very same people who take up guns and shoot at defenceless birds and deer who, when not killed, will escape to hide and die a slow, painful death...

Extract 2

I would like to point out that the fox population needs to be controlled now there are no natural enemies to control them. Shooting is not the answer, neither is poisoning which is the equivalent of indiscriminately murdering anything that moves. The outlawing of the hunt is not only bad for protected species but for the very survival of the countryside.

a) Which of the extracts is in favour of fox hunting?

b) What emotive words can you identify in the two extracts?

Extract 1:

Extract 2:

c) Make two lists from the extracts – one in favour of fox hunting; the other against.

In favour	Against

Answers to the self-check are at the end of the section.

Section summary

This section has been about learning to read critically in order to make your own decisions about information. It will also have helped you to start comparing information, ideas and opinions from different sources.

The previous sections have been mainly about increasing speed; this section has been an important part of increasing the quality of your reading.

Suggestions for Self-check 4

a)   Extract 2

b)   abuse, bemused, defenceless, slow painful death, murdering, very survival

c)

<table>
<tr><th>In favour</th><th>Against</th></tr>
<tr><td>Less cruel than shooting</td><td>No arguments against</td></tr>
<tr><td>Fox population needs to be controlled</td><td></td></tr>
<tr><td>Poisoning could kill other species</td><td></td></tr>
</table>

Hint
You may have been surprised that I wrote 'No arguments against' but the first article is against shooting foxes rather than against fox hunting.

Section 5: Using a library

Section 5: Using a library

Welcome to Section 5 of the 'Reading' module. In this section you will be looking at using a library. It's important to know how to do this. Libraries contain a lot of information. They have changed from the time when they just contained books and newspapers. Today most libraries have a wide range of resources that you can use, from reference books to the internet.

Although we can now access information in all kinds of different ways – on the internet and from the television – reading techniques are still just as important. In fact, it can be argued that because there is so much information around reading well is more important than ever. In this section you will also have an opportunity to practise your scanning and skimming techniques.

Topic 1: What is the best way to use a library?

In this topic you will look at how to use a library. The best way to use a library will depend on what you want from it. For example, you may require information or just to borrow a book for pleasure. Other things on offer could be the internet, magazines, newspapers, or local archives.

Reasons for completing this topic

This topic will help you to think about:

● how information can be organised and referenced in different ways

● how to use a library.

Looking for books

The range and level of the books and other items in a library will depend on its size and resources. For example, a large city library might offer a wide range of services and books. There will probably be a large section of **reference books** that you can read or refer to in the library but can't borrow. There may also be a wide range of specialist books or textbooks that can be borrowed. A local branch library might have a smaller range of books and resources. The stock will probably be mostly fiction or more popular non-fiction books such as DIY manuals.

It is important that you become familiar with the layout of libraries, as this will make it quicker for you to find information.

Books in a library are normally placed in a certain order or classification. The normal method of classification for **non-fiction** is the Dewey Decimal System. We will look at this next.

Dewey Decimal System

A young American librarian, Melvil Dewey, invented this system in 1876. He divided the field of human knowledge into ten major classes, to subdivide these classes into ten divisions, each division into ten sections, and so on.

Dewey's ten main classes are:

000 Generalities

100 Philosophy

200 Religion

300 Social sciences

400 Languages

500 Science

600 Applied science

700 Arts

800 Literature

900 History

Each of these ten classes is subdivided into ten divisions. Taking Science as an example:

500 Natural sciences

510 Mathematics

520 Astronomy

530 Physics

540 Chemistry

550 Earth sciences

560 Palaeontology

570 Life sciences

580 Botany

590 Zoology

Each of these divisions is further divided into ten sections. Physics, for example, is subdivided as follows:

530 Physics

531 Solid mechanics

532 Fluid mechanics

533 Gas mechanics

534 Sound

535 Light

536 Heat

537 Electricity

538 Magnetism

539 Modern physics

With the use of a decimal point, and extra digits after the point, each of these sections can be further subdivided to cover increasingly narrow subject areas. For example, for Electricity:

537.5   Electronics

537.534   Radio waves

537.5342 Long waves

537.5343 Short waves

The longer the class number, the more specialist the subject. The shorter the number, the more general it is. So, on the shelves you will find that the more general books come first in the sequence. As you move along the shelves, you will find the books becoming more specialised.

Books are then arranged alphabetically by surname of author.

In Activity 1 you will have an opportunity to go to a library to see how the system works in practice.

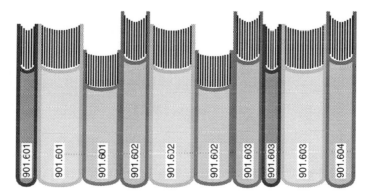

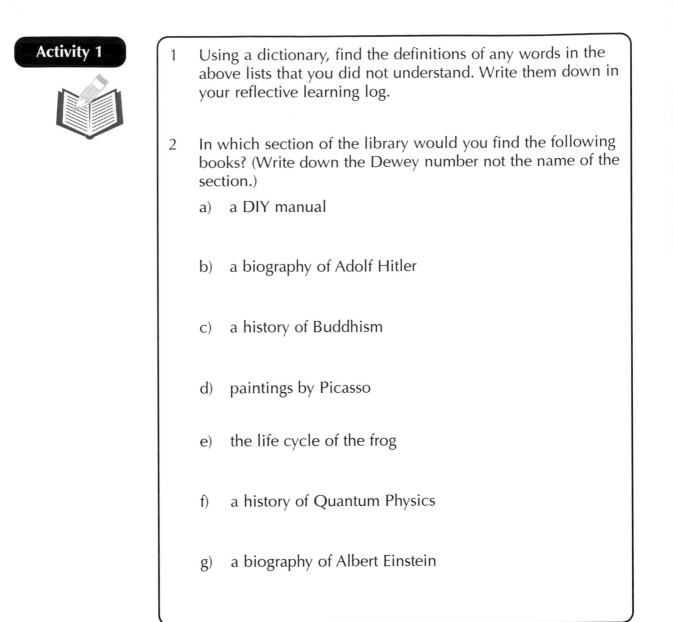

Activity 1

1   Using a dictionary, find the definitions of any words in the above lists that you did not understand. Write them down in your reflective learning log.

2   In which section of the library would you find the following books? (Write down the Dewey number not the name of the section.)

a)   a DIY manual

b)   a biography of Adolf Hitler

c)   a history of Buddhism

d)   paintings by Picasso

e)   the life cycle of the frog

f)   a history of Quantum Physics

g)   a biography of Albert Einstein

Suggestions for Activity 1

1   I hope you found it useful to find the definitions. If you need to, refer back to your definitions as you work through this section.

2   Your answers should look like this.

a)   000

b)   900

c)   200

d)   700

e)   500

f)   600

g)   100

This was not easy because some books come under sections that are not obvious. You would have to look under each heading in the library until you find the answer.

Also, fiction is usually arranged alphabetically by author rather than under the Dewey system.

Another way of finding a book is to look up its **ISBN** number. Each book has its own unique number. This acts like a car number plate – you can use it to trace a book. The ISBN number of this workbook is on the back of the title page.

Reference books

Reference books are books that can be read or photocopied in the library but are not available for loan. These are often an excellent place to start looking for information as they usually have a summary and recommendations for further reading. Encyclopaedias can be a particularly useful place to start if you are doing some research on a topic. Many libraries also have CD-Roms containing electronic versions of reference books.

Scanning and skimming books in a library

If you don't have the title or name of the author of a book, you may have to look through the books in the library until you find the one you want. This is where skimming and scanning will save you a lot of time and effort. You looked at scanning and skimming in Section 1.

First, you will need to find the section in the library where the book is most likely to be. For example, if you know it is a book about history you can go straight to the history shelves (starting with the number 900). There may be more than one book on the topic you are interested in. If you do not have the time to read each one, how can you decide which book is the one you need? Here are some steps to help you.

Hint

If you are looking for a book on a particular topic, don't spend long on this. Make your decision quickly. Why shouldn't you spend some time on this? Once you have put a book down, do not pick it up again.

Scanning and skimming books

● Decide which book to look at.

● Read the summary of the book on the back cover.

● Look at the date when it was published. Is it out of date? (Be careful it may be old but still relevant!)

● Look at the contents page. How many chapters are there and are most of them relevant to what you need?

● If you need a specific piece of information or a name, look in the index at the back.

● Read the first chapter heading.

● Read the first sentence of the first chapter. Is the book at the right level for you?

● Are there sub-headings?

● Are there summaries at the end of each chapter? If so, quickly read the summary at the end of the first chapter to see if it is going to give you what you need.

For the next activity you will need to visit a library. Activity 3 in Topic 2 also involves a visit to a library. If you have time, you might want to do both activities during one visit.

Activity 2

1   Go to a local library and find out:

● which of the following services they offer

● any costs they charge for the services.

Fill in the table below.

	Yes or No?	Cost?
Photocopying		
Access to the Internet		
Books to borrow		
Inter-library loans		
Reserved material		
Magazines and journals		
Newspapers		
Reference section		
Academic journals		

Activity 2 continued

2   Find the following information from the library's catalogue:

   a)   the name of a book by Arthur Miller

   b)   the title of a book on origami

   c)   what Gibbon's Catalogue deals with

3   Find the section on British History. Select two books and make a note of the following information.

	Book 1 **Title:**	**Book 2** **Title:**
year it was published		
level it is aimed (e.g. GCSE)		
ISBN number		
number of chapters		

   Are there any major differences between the books in terms of layout?

4   Using your scanning and skimming techniques, find a book on a topic that interests you. Make notes below.

   Title of book:

   What it is about:

   Level it is aimed at:

   Number of chapters:

   a)   If there is an index, find a person's name in the index and write it down below.

Activity 2 continued

b) Would you enjoy reading the book or would you find it useful (or both)? Give reasons for your answer.

5 In the reference section, find out the following information.

a) the date of the Battle of Trafalgar

b) the number of states in the USA

c) the names of the last ten British Prime Ministers including the present one

Hint

Make sure you leave the library with a user's guide to the library and any other information that you will find useful, such as opening times, how to reserve a book etc.

6 How long did this activity take you?

7 Do you think you would be able to complete it more quickly now you know your way around the library?

Suggestions for Activity 2

Your answers to most of the questions will depend on the library you visited and the books you looked at. I hope you found the visit helpful and that you feel that next time you will be able to find your way around more easily.

The answers to question 6 are:

a)   Battle of Trafalgar: 21 October 1805

b)   51

c)   Tony Blair; John Major; Margaret Thatcher; James Callaghan; Harold Wilson; Edward Heath; Alec Douglas-Home; Harold Macmillan; Anthony Eden; Winston Churchill.

Summary

> **Hint**
> Know what you want before you go to a library.

In Topic 1 you have looked at using a library to find information and seen how that information can be organized in different ways. Remember that most libraries – no matter how small or large – are organised the same way. Therefore the skills we have looked at above apply to all.

> By completing Topic 1 you have covered point 6 of the 'Text Focus' section of the Adult Literacy Core Curriculum: 'use organisational features and systems to locate texts and information'.

Topic 2: Finding magazines, newspapers and journals

In this second topic you will continue to look at how to use a library. We now move from books to looking for magazines, newspapers and journals.

Reasons for completing this topic

This topic will help you to be aware of what is available in a library apart from books.

Using other material in a library

Most libraries will have a range of other materials apart from books, which will be useful sources of information. In large libraries, there will often be a separate reference section. The range of material will depend on the size of the library, but most will have:

- information leaflets on a range of topics such as Employment, Health, Housing and Welfare Benefits
- business information
- local history material
- local community information – events, maps, bus/train timetables
- maps and atlases
- a range of national/local newspapers
- magazines and journals.

How these are set out will vary from library to library, so it is important to ask member of staff if you have a query or need help.

Information is also likely to be available via the Internet, CD-Roms and databases.

Items not immediately available can be requested. All libraries operate an inter-library loan service.

Magazines and newspapers

These are often more up to date than books because they are published on a more regular basis.

Special subject magazines

These will usually cover areas of special interest, such as mountain biking. They can be useful for up to date information, as specialists in the field probably wrote the articles.

Newspapers

Newspapers give up to date opinions. Different papers will often give two sides of an argument.

If you use magazines or newspapers to look for information use the same ways of scanning, skimming and reading in depth that was mentioned for books.

> **Hints**
> 1. Newspapers are a lot more difficult to use than other sources as they do not have detailed contents pages. Going through back numbers can be very time-consuming.
> 2. The librarian will know more than you about what information is where, so get into the habit of asking – don't struggle on your own.

The next activity involves a visit to library. You may be able to do Activity 2 from Topic 2 and this activity during one visit if you have time.

Activity 3

1   Make a list of five special interest magazines, two broad-sheet newspapers and two tabloid newspapers.

2   What themes or ideas do the magazines deal with? Select two of the magazines and say what themes or ideas they deal with.

Magazine 1

Magazine 2

3   What subjects do the main articles cover?

Magazine 1

Magazine 2

Activity 3 continued

4   What are the articles trying to do – amuse, inform, change your ideas, something else?

Magazine 1

Magazine 2

5   At which section of the population are the magazines aimed? How do you know?

Magazine 1

Magazine 2

6   Look at the advertisements in the magazine. How do you think are they designed to make people buy things?

Magazine 1

Magazine 2

7   Are the advertisements aimed at particular types of people and are these the same people the rest of the magazine is aimed at?

Magazine 1

Magazine 2

Activity 3 continued

> 8   Would you become a regular reader of each magazine? Give reasons for your answer.
>
>   Magazine 1
>
>
>
>   Magazine 2

Suggestions for Activity 3

Your answers will probably be different, depending on which magazines you selected.

Most magazines are aimed at a certain group. Obviously, a motorcycle magazine is aimed at people who own or want to own a motorcycle. Articles would be about types of motorbike, the best buy, and details of motorbike races that have taken place.

A magazine such as *Good Housekeeping* would be aimed at a different market. The language used would be different, and the advertising in that magazine would be directed towards people who own their own homes, are interested in DIY, and like fashion or cookery.

Reflective learning log

1.   Write down below three things you have learned about libraries by completing this section.

2.   Is there anything you would do differently next time you go to a library looking for information? Make notes in your learning log.

Summary

In Topic 2 you have looked at sources of information in libraries other than books. It is important to note that we have not looked at electronic information services which are widely available. To use these, ask the librarian.

> By completing Topic 2 you have covered points 5 and 6 of the 'Text Focus' section of the Adult Literacy Core Curriculum.

Topic 3: Using a dictionary and a thesaurus

In this topic, you will be using a **dictionary** and a **thesaurus**. In Section 1, we said that always stopping to use a dictionary will not make you an efficient reader. There will, however, be times when you are reading or writing when you will need to stop and check the meaning or spelling of a word.

Reasons for completing this topic

This topic will help you to use reference material to find the meaning of unfamiliar words.

Choosing the right dictionary/thesaurus

> **Hint**
> The biggest is not necessarily the best, as it could be at too high a level for what you need.

It is important that you use the right dictionary. There is a wide range on the market so if you are buying one go to a bookshop and skim and scan a selection. Look for:

● How it is laid out.

● Is it too simple for what you need?

● How much does it cost?

● How many entries does it have?

A thesaurus does not contain meanings of words, but it will give a list of words or phrases which mean the same as another. Look at the following example from *Roget's Thesaurus*:

blunder, mistake, misjudge, fail

A thesaurus is very useful when you need to find a word to replace another in a text.

Activity 4 will give you an opportunity to use a dictionary.

© National Extension College Trust Ltd

Activity 4

1   Using a dictionary, find 26 words, each beginning with a different letter of the alphabet and each having more than 10 letters. Write the words on a separate sheet of paper.

2   Find the meaning of the following words and write them down below.

alien	norm
brigand	opulent
climatic	perfect
denounce	quantities
epidermis	rhetoric
fauna	scallop
gargoyle	trcachery
holistic	ulna
imminent	vivacious
jewel	warrant
kinetic	xenon
logical	yodel
myriad	zygote

Suggestions for Activity 4

I found the following meanings in a dictionary. Some of them may be different from yours – if so, don't worry as different dictionaries give slightly different meanings.

alien – strange	norm – usual
brigand – robber	opulent – rich
climatic – concerning the weather	perfect – flawless
denounce – condemn	quantities – numbers
epidermis – outer layer of the skin	rhetoric – persuasive speaking
fauna – animal life	scallop – sea creature
gargoyle – church decoration	treachery – betrayal
holistic – total	ulna – a bone
imminent – about to happen	vivacious – lively
jewel – precious stone	warrant – deserve
kinetic – due to motion	xenon – a gas
logical – following a set pattern	yodel – type of singing
myriad – many	zygote – a human cell

Dictionary v. thesaurus

One problem with dictionaries is that they may only give you one definition of a word, or the definition they give does not fit into the text. For example, take the following sentence:

> The letters he sent were usually private, although a lot of people read them.

If you wanted to replace the word 'private' and looked it up in the dictionary you could end up with the following sentence:

> The letters he sent were usually not holding public office or official position although a lot of people read them.

This does not make sense.

What you need to look for is a word that means the same as 'private' – what we call a **synonym**.

The quickest way to do this is to use a thesaurus. Again, there is a wide range of these on the market. You will need to look through a few before you buy one, but it is worth buying one. A thesaurus will not give you definitions of words, but it will give you alternatives to words and even phrases. This is useful if you are making notes or summarising a text.

In the next activity you will have an opportunity to practise using a thesaurus.

Activity 5

Using a thesaurus, rewrite the following passage putting in the thesaurus version of the underlined words.

Uncle Albert was <u>irascible</u> and constantly upset the family with his <u>eccentric</u> behaviour.

A <u>typical</u> example was when we took him to a concert. He was totally <u>oblivious</u> to the <u>nuances</u> of the music and always fell asleep.

Not only did this <u>incense</u> us, it also <u>alienated</u> the audience as they were <u>debarred</u> from hearing the <u>dialogue</u> by his snoring!

Suggestions for Activity 5

Here are our suggestions – you may well have chosen other alternatives. Your new sentences should still make sense.

Uncle Albert was very <u>irritable</u> and constantly upset the family with his <u>strange</u> behaviour.

A <u>good</u> example was when we took him to a concert. He was totally unaware of the subtle <u>meaning</u> of the music and always fell asleep.

Not only did this <u>annoy</u> us, it also <u>upset</u> the audience as they were <u>prevented</u> from hearing the actors' words by his snoring!

We hope you found it helpful to use a thesaurus. Think about using one next time you are stuck for a word when you are writing.

Summary

Although this was a short section, it has given you some practice in using a dictionary and thesaurus to find the meanings of unfamiliar words.

Remember to use your dictionary as little as possible when reading intensely as it tends to interrupt your reading rhythm. But always have a good dictionary to hand and use it if it will help you.

Reflective learning log

Make a note of some of the things you have learned from Section 5. Write down anything about your reading that you think has improved as a result of working through this section. As you work through the rest of the module try to make a note in your learning log if you use the things you have learned in this section.

Self-check 5

Make a list of some of the possible places where you could expect to find the following information:

Information	Source(s)
Yesterday's cricket results	
The capital of Ethiopia	
Results of tests on new cars	
The Census for 1900	
Prices of second-hand caravans	
A novel by D. H. Lawrence	
Encyclopedia Britannica on CD-Rom	
List of local councillors	
Tomorrow's weather	
A textbook on GCSE Maths	

My suggestions for Self-check 5 are on the next page.

Section summary

Libraries are an important source of information on a wide range of topics. It is important that you feel confident using them. All libraries are different, but remember they are there to help people use them as much as possible. This section will hopefully have given you an introduction to using libraries. However, it has only scratched the surface. It is up to you to find out how useful libraries really are by going there often!

> By completing this topic you have covered points 2 and 3 of the 'Text Focus' section of the Adult Literacy Core Curriculum. It has also covered point 3 of 'Word Focus', on vocabulary.

Suggestions for Self-check 5

Here are my suggestions:

Information	Source(s)
Yesterday's cricket results	newspaper/internet
The capital of Ethiopia	library – atlas/reference book
Results of tests on new cars	car magazine/newspaper
The Census for 1900	library/internet
Prices of second-hand caravans	newspaper/specialist magazines
A novel by D. H. Lawrence	library/bookshop
Encyclopedia Britannica on CD-Rom	library
List of local councillors	library
Tomorrow's weather	newspaper
A textbook on GCSE Maths	library/bookshop

Section 6: Reading technical documents

Section 6: Reading technical documents

Welcome to the final section of this module. In this section you will be looking at reading technical documents. These can range from a simple guide to setting an alarm on a radio-controlled clock to a full company manual on the workings of a nuclear reactor. Reasons for reading technical material will also vary, from using the text as a simple guide to an action (e.g. programming a video) to having to understand the workings of a computer network system.

Topic 1: Looking at technical texts

This topic looks at what **technical texts** are and how to read them.

Reasons for completing this topic

This topic will help you to read and understand technical vocabulary.

What is a technical text?

Technical texts are written to pass on information clearly and effectively. If a technical text is not doing this, it is not doing its job.

A technical text should have a layout that includes:

- a table of contents
- section and sub-headings
- cross-references and **citations.**

These are signposts pointing the reader to what is important. They help the reader go straight to the section in which they are interested. Technical documents also tend to have graphs, charts and other illustrations.

Reading technical texts

When you are reading technical texts, the basic rules of reading that we have looked at in this module still apply:

- scanning
- skimming
- read in depth.

Technical texts should only contain relevant material and should have more signposts than a normal report when you are scanning and skimming.

Look for:

- bullet lists or numbered lists
- tables
- text in italics
- displays including
  - diagrams
  - pictures
  - graphs
- concrete examples.

Then read in depth.

Technical language

Hopefully, any technical material you need to read will not contain too much **jargon** or too many difficult technical terms. A good technical author will aim to use **plain English** and keep the text as easy to read as possible.

There are, however, bound to be a few technical words or phrases. If you come across a technical word that you do not understand, look up its meaning in a dictionary or a technical dictionary. Some technical texts also have a glossary explaining the words that are important to know in order to understand the text.

It is also worth trying to work out the meaning of a technical word. Technical words are often made up of other words. Computing is a good example where a new technical language has emerged with words such as 'megabyte' and 'pixel'.

If you are involved in a specific technical area, you will soon pick up the most common words and phrases. If you are new to the field, it is useful to start making lists of words and their meanings as you come across them.

Try using a dictionary to look up some technical words in the next activity.

Activity 1

Using a dictionary, find the meanings of the following technical words and write them below.

semiconductor

megabyte

hydrocarbon

telecommunications

coaxial

television

waveband

petrochemical

electromagnetism

glassfibre

Self-check 6 continued

2

To be sure of eating a well-balanced diet, you need to eat a variety of different foods each day:

- <u>Bread, other cereals and potatoes</u>
- <u>Fruit and vegetables</u>
- <u>Milk and dairy foods</u>
- <u>Meat, fish and alternatives</u>
- <u>Foods containing fat</u>
- <u>Foods containing sugar</u>.

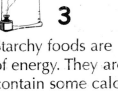
3

Starchy foods are rich in <u>carbohydrates</u>, an important source of energy. They are also a good source of B vitamins, and contain some calcium and iron. Starchy foods such as bread, cereals and potatoes should form the main part of your meals. Choose high-fibre varieties whenever you can.

4

Fruit and vegetables are an excellent source of vitamins and minerals. Try to eat at least five portions of fruit and vegetables each day. Include some fruit, some vegetables and some salad, and choose a wide variety to ensure you are getting all the vitamins and minerals you need. Dried fruit and fruit juice can make up some of the choices from this group.

5

Dairy foods are a good source of protein, calcium and vitamins A, D, and B12. They can also be high in saturated fat. Choose lower-fat versions whenever possible.

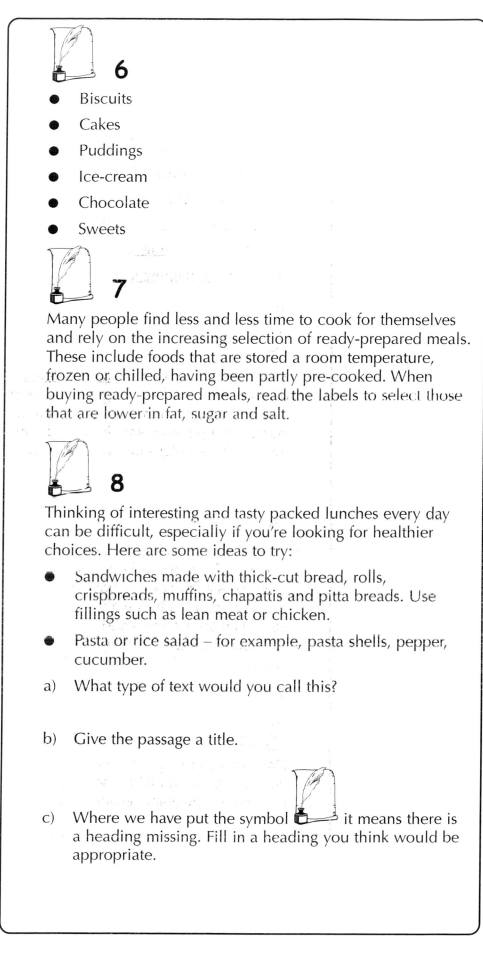

6

- Biscuits
- Cakes
- Puddings
- Ice-cream
- Chocolate
- Sweets

7

Many people find less and less time to cook for themselves and rely on the increasing selection of ready-prepared meals. These include foods that are stored a room temperature, frozen or chilled, having been partly pre-cooked. When buying ready-prepared meals, read the labels to select those that are lower in fat, sugar and salt.

8

Thinking of interesting and tasty packed lunches every day can be difficult, especially if you're looking for healthier choices. Here are some ideas to try:

- Sandwiches made with thick-cut bread, rolls, crispbreads, muffins, chapattis and pitta breads. Use fillings such as lean meat or chicken.

- Pasta or rice salad – for example, pasta shells, pepper, cucumber.

a)   What type of text would you call this?

b)   Give the passage a title.

c)   Where we have put the symbol ▨ it means there is a heading missing. Fill in a heading you think would be appropriate.

By completing Section 6 you have covered the points 1 and 2 of the 'Word Focus' section of the Adult Literacy Core Curriculum:

- 'read and understand technical vocabulary'

- 'use reference material to find the meaning of unfamiliar words'.

Suggestions for Self-Check 6

1 a) Persuasive

b) I would suggest 'HEALTHY EATING'.

c) I would suggest:

1 – Guidelines for Healthy Eating

2 – A Well Balanced Diet

3 – Starchy Foods

4 – Fruit and Vegetables

5 – Dairy Foods

6 – Snacks

7 – Ready Prepared Meals

8 – Packed Lunches

d) This passage is mainly about what you need to do to make sure what you eat is healthy. It recommends you to eat a well-balanced diet. You need to eat lots of fruit and vegetables and dairy foods but not too many biscuits, cakes or other sweet foods.

2 a) This article disagrees with the text in Self-check 6 question 1. It is against the idea of anyone telling other people how to live their lives.

b) It is biased because the author:

➤ uses emotive words

➤ does not try to see the other person's point of view.

Points to note:

Text 1 could, at first glance, be seen as a descriptive document because it does not seem to have a point of view and is full of good advice.

The author of Text 2 is obviously a smoker and wants to get his/her case over to other people which would make the text persuasive.

You must remember, however, that the author(s) of the first text are pushing a point of view just as strongly as the second. They strongly believe in the idea of healthy eating and want to change the way other people eat.

While the second article uses stronger and more emotional language, he/she is only putting a point over. It could be argued that as the message of the article is that everyone must be left to make their own decisions, the author is not trying to convert anyone to his/her point of view.

If you have different opinions on the material, don't worry. If you are challenging what you read we have done a decent job in training you to be a good reader!

Glossary

Glossary

The following terms all feature in the 'Reading' module. As they are key terms, they appear in the text in **bold**. The definitions relate to the use of each term in this module.

active reader	someone who thinks about a piece of writing before and during reading rather than just reading the words
appendices	extra information that is placed after the end of the main text (singular: appendix)
argument	statements in support of an opinion; used to convince someone else that the opinion is correct
audience	the people addressed by a text. The term includes listeners, readers of print, film/TV audiences, and users of information technology.
author	person who wrote a piece of writing
bias	when an author writes a text which only gives one side of an argument. Information will often be presented in an unfair way.
bibliography	list of books and other reference material (often including websites) on a particular subject
broadsheet	in British English, a newspaper or advertisement that is printed on one large sheet of paper. Examples: *The Times* and *Daily Telegraph*. Opposite is a **tabloid**.
citations	quotations from books or other pieces of writing
descriptive text	piece of writing, such as a book, magazine or article, which describes things or people
Dewey Decimal System	one way books in a library can be classified. Each book is given a number depicting the classification into which it fits. Melvil Dewey invented the system in 1876.
dictionary	a book in which the words of a language are listed alphabetically and their meanings are explained
editorials	articles in newspapers and the like which give the opinion of the editor or publisher on a topic or item of news

e-mail   short for 'electronic mail'; messages sent electronically from computer to computer

emotive language   words, which are written or spoken to make people feel strongly about something

explanatory text   writing, such as a DIY manual, which instructs how to do things

formal text   writing where the style of language is determined by a distance from the audience (e.g. a letter from a Bank Manager or the Inland Revenue). The letter should start 'Dear Sir/Madam' and end 'Yours faithfully'.

glossary   list of words or expressions, in alphabetical order, and the special meanings that they have. You are reading the glossary definition for the term as used in this module.

index   alphabetical list that is usually printed at the back of a text to show you where particular subjects, people, places, events etc. are in the publication

informal text   writing, such as a letter from a friend, where the choice of words is determined by a connection with the audience. Tends not have long words and phrases.

ISBN   International Standard Book Number. Each book that is published is given a unique ISBN. The 10 digits contain information about the country of origin, the publisher, edition and title.

jargon   terms that are used in special or technical ways, usually used when talking about particular subjects, e.g. megabyte and pixel are computing jargon.

journalists   people who work on a newspaper or magazine and write articles for it

key words   the words that carry the substance of a phrase or the meaning of a sentence. Identifying the key words of a text is therefore a means of understanding its gist.

layout   way in which the parts are arranged, e.g. the way this Glossary has been laid out by the designer on this page

messages   pieces of information that you send to someone or leave somewhere for them when you cannot speak directly; could be in the form of a memo, letter, email or text message.

methodology   system of methods and principles for doing something (e.g. for teaching or for carrying out research)

non-fiction   writing that is based on fact and truth rather than a story or an account that has been invented

note taking   process of writing down important points quickly, so that you can refer to them later

novel   long story written about people and events that have been invented by the author

paragraph   section of a piece of writing. A new paragraph marks a change of focus, a change of place or a change of speakers in a passage or dialogue. A new paragraph begins on a new line.

persuasive text   texts that try to persuade the reader by stating a point of view and giving arguments and evidence to support that point of view

Plain English   writing in English using clearly understood words in order to communicate information in a simpler way

prejudice   where someone has an unfair attitude to another person or group of people

reading for a purpose   knowing what you want from writing while you are reading it – similar to active reading

reading in depth   reading texts in detail to get information

reference books   publications such as dictionaries and encyclopedias that contain detailed information, often about a particular subject

report   written or spoken account of something that has happened; also an official document prepared officially

scanning   looking through a text very quickly, to find information by locating a key word

sections   separate points into which something has been divided, e.g. this course module is divided into seven sections

sensational words   language used in a way that is intended to produce strong feelings of shock, anger or frustration. Similar to **emotive language.**

signposts   things in texts used to give you an idea of which parts are important: bold letters, italics, bullet points

skimming	looking at headings, first paragraphs, contents page etc. of long texts to get an initial overview of the subject matter and main ideas
summarising	condensing material into a shorter form while still retaining the overall meaning and main points. The written form is sometimes a *précis*.
summary	short written or spoken account of something, which gives the important points but not the details
synonym	word that has the same meaning (in a particular context) as another word, e.g. big and large
tabloid	small-sized newspaper or the like, in which the news stories and articles are short, usually with a lot of photographs
technical texts	material that has a particular meaning that depends on the (usually, working) context in which they are used; may include **jargon**
terms of reference	the limits given to someone when they are asked to consider or investigate a particular subject. These limits tell them what they must deal with and what they can ignore.
text	pieces of writing – can be anything from a short note to a long book
text message	word messages that are sent using a mobile telephone
thesaurus	dictionary which gives words with the same meanings as others